# Conservation Heroes

# CHICO MENDES

# Conservation Heroes

Ansel Adams

John James Audubon

Rachel Carson

Jacques Cousteau

Jane Goodall

Al Gore

Steve and Bindi Irwin

Chico Mendes

John Muir

Theodore Roosevelt

# Conservation Heroes

# CHICO MENDES

Alexa Gordon Murphy

CHELSEA HOUSE
*An Infobase Learning Company*

Chelsea House
An imprint of Infobase Learning
132 West 31st Street
New York, NY 10001

**Library of Congress Cataloging-in-Publication Data**
Murphy, Alexa Gordon.
    Chico Mendes / by Alexa Gordon Murphy.
        p. cm. — (Conservation heroes)
    Includes bibliographical references and index.
    ISBN 978-1-60413-951-8 (hardcover)
    1. Mendes, Chico, d. 1988–   —Juvenile literature. 2. Conservationists—
Brazil—Biography—Juvenile literature. 3. Rubber tappers—Brazil—Biography—
Juvenile literature. 4. Rain forest conservation—Amazon River Region—Juvenile
literature. 5. Deforestation—Control—Amazon River Region—Juvenile
literature. I. Title.
    SD411.52.M46M87 2011
    333.72092—dc22
    [B]                                                                      2010030590

Text design by Annie O'Donnell
Cover design by Takeshi Takahashi
Composition by Newgen North America
Cover printed by Yurchak Printing, Landisville, Penn.
Book printed and bound by Yurchak Printing, Landisville, Penn.
Date printed: April 2011
Printed in the United States of America

10 9 8 7 6 5 4 3 2 1

This book is printed on acid-free paper.

# Contents

1 A Stranger in the Forest 7

2 Birth and Childhood 17

3 The Forest Is Threatened 28

4 Organizing the Rubber Tappers 41

5 Lighting the Way 52

6 Bringing the Cause to the World 60

7 Progress and Retaliation 72

8 Chico Mendes's Legacy 94

How to Get Involved 109

Chronology 111

Glossary 113

Bibliography 114

Further Resources 118

Picture Credits 120

Index 121

About the Author 126

# A Stranger in the Forest

The year was 1960, and the day started out like any other for 14-year-old Chico Mendes and his family. They were *seringueiros,* which means "rubber tappers," who lived in the Amazon rain forest in Brazil. They lived on a rubber estate and spent their days collecting latex from trees in the forest and selling it to the estate owner for rubber production.

Most rubber tappers in those days could not read, write, or even count. Schools were not allowed on the rubber estates. The rubber estate owners knew that if the rubber tappers learned to read, write, and do math, they might figure out that they were not being paid fairly for their work. Thus, Chico did not go to school. Instead, he began tapping rubber with his father when he was nine years old. His father could read and count a little and taught Chico what he knew, but there was little time for education in the life of a rubber tapper.

Then, one day in 1960, Chico's fortunes changed. He and his father had just returned from collecting latex from the rubber trees in the forest and were at work outside their house, curing

## Amazon Rain Forest

the latex over a wood fire, when a man approached their house. Chico's father had met the man at the company store a few days previously and invited him to visit his home. The man stopped and began to chat with the Mendes family. He was a rubber tapper, but he was different from the rest. He looked and spoke differently, and he carried newspapers with him. Although Chico couldn't read and had never seen a newspaper before, he was curious. Sensing his interest, the man invited Chico to visit him in his home and offered to teach him how to read. Chico's father agreed to let him take time off from work each weekend to visit the man in his hut.

And so it began. Each Saturday afternoon, Chico would walk the narrow path through the rain forest to the man's hut. The walk took three hours, and Chico would spend the night. "I was so interested in what he had to say that at times I spent the whole night awake, listening to him," Chico said in his autobiography.

After they had known each other for a year, the man began to tell Chico about himself. His name was Euclides Fernandes Távora. He was working as a rubber tapper, but he told Chico that he was really a revolutionary in hiding. He was the son of a prominent family from southern Brazil. He had been an officer in the army and, in 1935, he joined the Communist revolution in Brazil, which was led by Luis Carlos Prestes. Prestes attempted a military coup in 1935, but the revolt failed, and many members of the movement, including Távora, were arrested and put in prison on the island of Fernando de Noronha. Távora managed to escape and joined another rebellion, but was arrested again. After this,

*(continues on page 12)*

(opposite page) Sixty percent of the Amazon rain forest is in Brazil. The Amazon makes up the largest tropical rain forest in the world—and it is filled with the world's largest collection of diverse plants, animals, and insects.

# BRAZIL IN BRIEF

Brazil is a country with a long and troubled history. The land was first settled in the 1500s by the Portuguese, who declared it a colony of Portugal. In 1822, the son of the Portuguese king declared the colony to be independent from Portugal and crowned himself Peter I, emperor of Brazil. The monarchy was overthrown in 1889, and a republic was established by the military. The country

The tropical rain forest in Brazil (*shown here*) produces about 3,000 fruits, including pineapples, bananas, avocados, tomatoes, coconuts, figs, grapefruits, oranges, lemons, guavas, and mangos. Also found there are hundreds of spices, including cinnamon, black pepper, cloves, ginger, and sugar cane, as well as nuts, such as cashews and Brazil nuts.

remained mostly under dictatorship and military rule until civilian rule was finally established in 1985.

Today, Brazil is the largest country in Latin America—home to nearly half of its people and land. Thanks to Portugal's colonization of Brazil and later immigration from Europe, about 54 percent of the country's population is of European descent. About 44 percent are of African descent, a result of the slave trade (slavery was abolished in Brazil in 1888). Less than one percent of Brazil's population is part of an indigenous group, and most of these groups live in the Amazon region. The country is divided into 26 states and 1 federal district. Brazil is considered Latin America's leading economic power, boasting vast natural resources and strong industrial development.

The Amazon rain forest region is Brazil's largest area, but it has the fewest number of people living in it. Brazilians have struggled to balance the need to gain economic benefit from this vast area with the need to protect the environment and the indigenous groups that live there.

**BRAZIL IN THE TWENTY-FIRST CENTURY:**
- Capital: Brasilia
- Population: Approximately 198,739,269, ranking 5th in the world
- Literacy rate: 88.6% over the age of 15 can read and write
- Official language: Portuguese
- Official religion: Catholic

**Source:** *CIA World Fact Book–Brazil*, September 2010.
*https://www.cia.gov/library/publications/the-world-factbook/geos/br.html*

(continued from page 9)

he escaped to Bolivia, a small country to the west of Brazil, where he was active in the struggle for workers' rights in the 1950s and the movement that opposed the government there. When the government began to crack down on the opposition movement, Távora escaped arrest and fled into the jungle, where he made his way over the border to Brazil.

Because they had no textbooks, Távora taught Chico to read and write using the only printed material they had available to them: newspapers. Even these were not easy to get, and were several months old by the time they made their way to Távora's hut in the rain forest. Learning to read from these materials helped Chico understand much more than the skill of literacy. He was being taught what was happening in the world outside the rubber estate, and he began to understand that the rubber tappers were not treated fairly.

When Chico and Távora first met, Brazil was governed by the democratically elected president Joao Goulart. Goulart was a populist whose sympathies were with rural workers. Under his regime, the labor force in Brazil began to organize and the first trade unions for rural workers were established. This was at the height of the Cold War, and conservative politicians and military leaders both inside and outside of Brazil feared that these changes would lead to the establishment of communism in Brazil. In 1964, with the support of the United States, conservative forces and the military carried out a coup d'etat and installed a dictatorship.

Chico and Távora listened to three radio programs that were transmitted from abroad. At around 5:00 P.M., they turned on a broadcast from Radio Moscow, which gave the communist perspective on world events, followed by Air America, and then a broadcast from the British Broadcasting Corporation in London. In the 1989 book *Fight for the Forest*, Mendes recalled listening to these broadcasts with his teacher and discussing the differing viewpoints each program offered. Voice of America considered the coup a great victory against communism in Brazil, but Radio Moscow condemned the oppression imposed by the new military regime. They also heard reports of repression against those opposing the new regime. Many

Rubber tappers slash the bark of trees in a pattern to draw sap (latex) from them.

opponents were being exiled or arrested, tortured, or assassinated—
and some of them simply disappeared. Yet Voice of America continued to celebrate the coup as a victory for democracy. Chico and
Távora would listen to the programs and then compare and discuss
the different versions of the story, trying to get at the truth and what
it all meant.

Meanwhile, the new regime established a new economic order
for Brazil, focused on promoting rapid industrialization by offering
foreign companies inexpensive labor in a politically stable country.
They achieved this by controlling wages and suppressing any opposition with brutal force.

Chico Mendes poses at age 44. He grew up in a family of rubber
tappers in Acre, Brazil, and began work as a rubber tapper by age
nine.

## BIODIVERSITY IN THE AMAZON

The Amazon rain forest is a vast area, covering more than 2.4 million square miles (3,286,427 square kilometers). Because of the constant hot temperatures, high humidity, and frequent rainfall, the Amazon is home to an incredible range of plants and animals. In fact, the Amazon is home to the largest range of plants and animals in the world. This range of species is what scientists refer to as biodiversity. One in ten of the known species on Earth makes its home in the Amazon. Scientists have classified tens of thousands of plant species and thousands of fish, mammals, and birds. It is believed that this covers only a small fraction of the species living in the Amazon.

Chico recalled that the time spent listening to the news with Távora "made me much more aware." Távora encouraged the teen to get involved in opposing the new regime, particularly in the trade union movement. "He gave me a lot of advice about how to organize in the trade union movement," Chico explained in his autobiography. Távora predicted that at least a decade or more of dictatorship lay ahead for Brazil, but he urged the teen not to give up hope for the opposition movement because it would always exist, even if it stayed beneath the surface. "He told me that nobody had ever been able to eliminate this movement for liberation in the world," noted Chico, who took this message to heart. He considered it a "prophecy about our country's future."

Chico lost touch with Távora after 1965, but he didn't forget the important lessons he learned from him. Just a few years later, he went on to help organize the first union for rubber tappers and became a leader in their struggle to maintain their way of life in the rain forest. He led the fight against powerful landowners and government forces and worked tirelessly to protect the rain forest from deforestation by cattle ranchers. Like his friend and teacher, he faced arrest and persecution, but he never gave up—even when his life was threatened.

Thanks to the tireless efforts of Chico Mendes and his comrades, many lives have been saved and many acres of rain forest have been protected from certain destruction. Would any of this have happened if Euclides Távora had not taught the teen how to read and write? It's hard to say. One thing is sure: Chico Mendes is a symbol of the fight to save the rain forest.

# Birth and Childhood

The story of Chico Mendes actually starts well before he was born, with the story of rubber tapping in the rain forests of Brazil. Indigenous people of the Amazon (Indians) had been harvesting latex, the creamy liquid found underneath the bark of rubber trees, for centuries. Using methods passed from generation to generation, they knew how to extract latex without damaging the trees, and they used it to waterproof their bags and shoes. In the 1700s, European travelers began taking rubber back to Europe with them, where it was used to make a variety of products ranging from waterproof clothing to surgical equipment. During this period, traders from towns along the Amazon River would make trips up its tributaries to collect latex from the Indian groups that lived there.

In the late 1800s, demand for latex increased in Europe and North America due to the invention of the rubber tire and other products. The Indian groups who had been supplying the traders could not produce enough to meet the demand, so traders began to bring poor workers from other areas into the Amazon to collect latex.

The traders took over areas of the forest and established the first rubber estates, which were known as *seringals*. The workers that were brought to these estates to become rubber tappers lived under a system of debt bondage. The rubber tappers were required to sell the latex they collected to the estate owners at artificially low prices. If they were caught selling this crude rubber to other merchants, they were severely and harshly punished—sometimes even killed.

The first rubber tappers were not allowed to grow their own food, and they were forced to purchase food from the estate store at very high prices. When the rubber tappers sold their latex to the owners, the price of the food and supplies the tappers had purchased was subtracted from the payment. They almost always owed more to the trading post than they earned selling rubber. They were not allowed to leave the rubber estate until their debt was paid off, but the system made it almost impossible for them to do so. Since the rubber tappers could not read, write, or count, they had no way of knowing whether they were being paid fairly.

This system flourished and became very profitable, with Great Britain controlling most of the rubber trade. This changed in the early 1900s, when rubber trees were exported to the British colony of Malaya and large rubber plantations were created there. After this, the international demand for Brazilian rubber fell dramatically for many years.

## SOLDIERS OF RUBBER

The rubber industry in Brazil was revived during World War II when Britain lost control of Malaya and no longer had access to the cheap rubber produced on the plantations there. These years are known in Brazil as the "rubber boom years." To meet the increased demand, a new group of rubber tappers was recruited from the poor areas of Brazil to come to the Amazon to tap rubber. They were called *soldados da boirracha,* or "rubber soldiers." Chico Mendes's father, Francisco Mendes, was among them.

# OTHER RESOURCES OF THE FOREST

Latex from rubber trees isn't the only natural resource the rain forest offers. As native groups living in the rain forest have known for centuries, the countless plant species growing there offer many uses, including the following:

**Food:** According to Rain-tree.com, 80 percent of the world's diet originated in the tropical rain forest. Many popular fruits (such as avocados, coconuts, pineapples, and tomatoes), grains and vegetables (corn, potatoes, rice, and yams), nuts (such as Brazil nuts and cashews), spices (black pepper, chocolate, cinnamon, ginger, and sugar cane), and coffee and vanilla beans grow naturally there.

**Medicinal plants:** Native peoples of the rain forest have used plants to cure various ailments for centuries, and Western medicine is finally catching on. For example, vincristine, a drug extracted from the periwinkle plant native to the rain forest, is a powerful anticancer drug. In fact, the U.S. National Cancer Institute has, as of now, identified 3,000 plants that have anticancer potential, and more than a third of these are native to the rain forest. Today, many pharmaceutical companies and the U.S. government are researching the potential of various rain forest plants for possible cures for viruses, infections, cancer, and even AIDS.

Just think of all the gifts the rain forest has provided to humans—and this potential has only begun to be tapped! However, these gifts will only be available to us if we leave the forest intact. Although rain forests once covered 14 percent of the earth, they now cover only 6 percent due to deforestation for ranching, logging, and development.

Francisco Mendes and his family were from the coastal state of Ceará in northeastern Brazil. This area had been plagued by drought and poverty, and many Brazilians fled in the 1920s to seek a better life elsewhere. The Mendes family first went to the Brazilian state of Pará and tried farming for about four years. In 1926, they travelled by boat to the Brazilian state of Acre to seek their fortunes as rubber tappers. When they arrived, they settled on a rubber estate near Xapuri, a small village near the Bolivian border, and entered into the system of debt bondage described earlier. Chico's father later married Iraci Lopes Filho, whose father and grandfather had also been rubber tappers. Yet Francisco Mendes was one of few rubber tappers who knew how to read.

## AN ACTIVIST IS BORN

Chico, whose full name was Francisco Alves Mendes, was born on December 15, 1944. He was the oldest of 17 siblings, only 6 of whom survived into adulthood.

The life of a rubber tapper was generally a life of hard work and extreme poverty, and the Mendes family was no exception. In addition to tapping rubber six days a week, they hunted for meat in the forest (from animals such as porcupine, armadillos, and monkey) and grew subsistence crops just to survive. They also harvested and sold Brazil nuts to increase their meager income.

Rubber tappers lived in simple homes deep in the forest, and groups of them were generally isolated from one another. This was partly because of the distance between each home—it took up to an hour or more walk to the nearest one. In addition, the estate owners promised rewards for rubber tappers to spy on one another and report to the boss if anyone tried to sell their rubber to another source. Because of this, the rubber tappers were unable to trust or rely on one another for support.

Despite the hardships and isolation, rubber tappers did occasionally come together for parties on the estate. Many of these parties were organized by the boss and took place at the trading post. Some

Rubber tapping has been a commercial industry for hundreds of years. In this December 1942 image, a large group of rubber tappers march up a hill to their group housing.

of these parties celebrated religious holidays and included religious rituals, such as saying a rosary or a mass. These celebrations would last all night long, with music and dancing. Some rubber tappers had to walk more than 10 hours in a day to attend a party, so these occasions were rare.

Chico began helping his father with his work when he was around eight years old. As previously noted, schools were not allowed on the rubber estates. Keeping children out of school helped the estate owners in two ways: First, they wanted to keep

An expert tapper shows others how to tap a rubber tree in this 1942 image.

their workers uneducated in both writing and math so they wouldn't know that the estate owners were cheating them. Second, since the children didn't go to school, they generally went to work with their parents at an early age, which increased production and profits for the estate owners.

Each rubber tapper had his own trail that looped through the forest and back to his home. Along each path were up to 200 rubber trees, which grow naturally in the rain forest. Rubber tappers had to walk 8 to 11 miles (12 to 17 km) each day to collect enough latex to survive.

Every morning Chico and his father awoke before dawn, and, after a quick breakfast, set out along their path. At each rubber tree, they stopped and made a slanted cut in the bark with a hooked knife. Then they attached cups, cans, or Brazil nut shells to the trunk to collect the latex that would pour out. When they were deep in the forest, they would hunt for meat to feed the family. Then, in the afternoon, they returned on the same path, collecting the latex from each tree they had tapped in the morning.

This method of harvesting latex from rubber trees does not harm the tree. After rubber tappers have made cuts on one entire side of a tree, they leave it alone to heal for about two years. Trees that are taken care of in this way remain healthy and alive in the forest for a far longer period of time than humans. This means that rubber tapping is a sustainable practice—a way to use the vast resources the rain forest offers without permanently harming the forest itself.

Once the latex was collected from the trees, Chico and his father would return home to cure it and prepare it for sale. The traditional method of curing latex in the rain forest involves pouring the latex into a spit over an open fire. As the spit is turned over the fire, the latex hardens into a large rubbery ball, which is then sold to the estate owner. Each ball weighs about 110 pounds (49.8 kilograms). The fumes from these curing fires are irritating and harmful, and lung disease is not uncommon among rubber tappers.

During the rainy season in December and January, it becomes very difficult to harvest latex from the trees, and so most rubber tappers harvest Brazil nuts during that time. Brazil nut trees are some of the tallest trees in the forest. They produce large fruits, about the size of a grapefruit, which fall to the forest floor when ripe. Brazil nut harvesters must be careful not to get hit by the falling fruits, which have been described as falling like cannonballs from high up in the trees. Inside each fruit are 12 to 25 Brazil nuts in individual shells. Brazil nut harvesting is almost as important to the Amazon's economy as rubber, and many forest dwellers divide their time between harvesting these two resources.

After rubber trees' sap is released, the harvesters collect the crude rubber. Here, native workers carry three large balls of crude rubber across a river by canoe.

## OVERCOMING FEARS AND GROWING UP

The walk through the forest is not without dangers—rubber tappers have to be alert for poisonous plants, snakes, and other dangerous animals lurking in the forest. When Chico was a child, his biggest fear was running into a jaguar. According to his friend Gomercindo Rodrigues, Chico would walk on tiptoe through the forest for fear of disturbing these large predatory cats. His father tried to teach him to use a gun so he would feel safer, but young Chico was so afraid that he would close his eyes while he aimed the gun.

Chico would sometimes bring along a dog as a companion for his rubber-tapping work. The dog would startle whenever he caught the scent of a jaguar and alert Chico to danger. The two of them would then run away in a panic. However, the need to survive in the rain forest doesn't allow for much indulgence of these types of fears.

Jaguars are among many wild animals in the Amazon that can be a hindrance to rubber tappers.

By the time he was 15, Chico had learned to shoot a gun properly and overcame his fear of jaguars. He began hunting for food for his family—even at night.

## SPOTLIGHT ON JAGUARS

Jaguars are the largest of the big cats native to South America. They can grow to up to six feet long and weigh anywhere from 100 to 300 pounds (45.3 to 136 kg). These predators once roamed from the southern tip of South America into northern Mexico and the southwestern United States, but they are now primarily found only in a few remote parts of the Amazon river basin in South and Central America.

The distinct spotted markings of the jaguar, which are actually rosettes and not true spots like a leopard's, help the cats hide among the grass, bushes, and trees in the rain forest, grasslands, and other woodlands that make up its natural habitat. Jaguars are nocturnal hunters that ambush their prey and crush their skulls with their powerful jaws. Because they can climb and swim, few animals of the forest are inaccessible to the jaguar. Their prey includes more than 85 different species, ranging in size from birds to deer.

Female jaguars have litters of one to four cubs and are fiercely protective of their offspring. Cubs stay with their mothers for their first two years, learning to hunt and survive in the wild. Jaguars typically live 12 to 15 years in the wild.

As a top predator of the rain forest, jaguars' main threat has come from humans. They have been hunted for their beautiful coats for decades. In the 1960s and 1970s, more than 15,000 jaguars were killed each year just for their fur. They have also lost much of their habitat to ranchers and other developers, and are still often shot by ranchers out of fear or the need to protect their livestock. Today, it is believed that only 15,000 jaguars survive in the wild.

When Chico was 17, his mother died during childbirth. Chico's father took over the job of tending the family's vegetable crops, and Chico helped take care of his younger brothers and sisters while tapping rubber six days a week. This left little time for fun, but occasionally his strict father allowed him to attend parties with his cousins.

Even in his teenage years, before meeting his teacher, Euclides Távora, Chico Mendes was aware that the rubber tappers were treated unfairly by the estate owners. He wanted to learn to read and write so he could understand the accounting methods that the estate owners used to keep his and so many other families in debt. As a teenager, he even wrote a letter (dictated to his father) to the president of Brazil, complaining about the conditions on the rubber estates. When Távora arrived in the early 1960s, Chico was eager to learn everything he could from him and, for the next four years, devoted his weekends to doing just that.

Távora encouraged Chico to become active in the movement to defend workers' rights, and Mendes didn't forget his advice. Over the next several years, as the rubber tappers' way of life became threatened by encroaching cattle ranches, Mendes took up the fight to protect his family's livelihood—and the forest.

# The Forest Is
# Threatened

In the late 1960s and early 1970s, the government of Brazil developed a new policy for developing the Amazon region economically. At the time, Brazil had a soaring national debt, and the military regime was looking for ways to generate revenue to pay it down. As a result, the government began to look toward the Amazon region for its economic potential.

Despite the vast natural resources available in the rain forest, the rubber-tapping industry, and the native people who lived there, the region was seen as an economic wasteland that could be put to better use by clearing the forest for farming and development. At the same time, the government wanted this largely unpopulated frontier to be settled in order to help protect the country's borders. According to Mendes's friend Gomercindo Rodrigues, in his book *Walking the Forest with Chico Mendes,* the military government also hoped to move many poor, unemployed people from the overcrowded urban centers to the remote Amazon, where they would be less able to organize against the regime.

With these two goals in mind, the government began a campaign to attract land speculators, ranchers, farmers, and other settlers to the region. The Superintendency for the Development of the Amazon (SUDAM) was established in 1966 to offer grants to land speculators for clearing the rain forest for development. Unemployed Brazilians were urged to move north, with the promise of land to farm, housing, health care, and a better life.

New highways were built leading to this previously remote region of Brazil, with devastating effects. With the roads came an influx of thousands of people from the southern part of Brazil. These included small farmers, rural workers, and unemployed people from the urban areas in central and southern Brazil. Their migration has been compared to the westward migration that occurred in the United States during the 1800s. Instead of gold, however, Brazilians moving into the Amazon were chasing fertile land and dreams of becoming wealthy cattle ranchers and landowners. The government set up settlements for the new arrivals and promised them houses, medical care, fertile land for farming, and schools for their children.

However, the reality for the new settlers in the Amazon was far from the dreams promised by the government. The settlers were given small plots of land to clear and farm, but the land became infertile once it was cleared. Certain areas quickly became overcrowded, and the combination of clearing large plots of land for farming along with the extreme increase in population resulted in the spread of diseases such as malaria, yellow fever, and hepatitis. With the failure of farming in the region, there were few other jobs available, so the people who had fled poverty in the south were now faced with even worse living conditions than what they had left behind. Cities rapidly cropped up in the Amazon and became extremely overcrowded in just a few years. Many of these poor settlers were forced into urban slums, with little or no hope of finding work.

In addition to attracting the urban poor to settle the Amazon, the government worked to lure large-scale cattle ranchers to the region by offering grants and incentives for purchasing and clearing large plots of land for development. At the same time, many of the rubber-estate owners were deeply in debt and welcomed the opportunity to sell their land. They eagerly sold their estates to the land speculators and cattle ranchers. Nobody thought much about the rubber tappers and other people who lived in the forest. The estate owners just wanted to sell the land and get out of debt. The new owners were mostly powerful businessmen from the southern part of Brazil who had even less regard for the people living on their new land—let alone the wildlife.

In some areas, the new owners never did anything with the land. Instead, they bribed the inspectors to report that they had developed a ranch so they could get the grant money from SUDAM. However, in Acre, the state Chico Mendes was from, the land was better for ranching than other parts of the Amazon. Ranchers began aggressively buying up rubber estates and clearing the land for pasture.

## SLASH AND BURN

When the rubber-estate lands were sold off to the ranchers, it had devastating effects on both the rubber tappers and the forest itself. Although many of the rubber tappers had legal rights to the land they had been working for years, it was virtually impossible to fight the powerful new landowners. The landowners forged and altered deeds and obtained title to land regardless of whether they had a legal right to it. They stole land from both indigenous groups and rubber tappers who had lived there for decades.

Poor and illiterate, most of the rubber tappers did not understand their rights or have the resources to navigate the legal system to gain title to the land. "Don't you sign anything!" Chico told the rubber tappers, according to Jorge Cappato in his article, "Who Was Chico Mendes," published on the Global 500 Forum Web site. "This land is ours. When you change it into money, you are losing the possibility of surviving. Land is life!" Nevertheless, the ranchers

This home of a Brazilian rubber tapper, shown in 1987, is somewhat typical of many rubber tappers' homes. Located near Xapuri, the wooden structure houses a couple and their 12 children, who sleep on hammocks in their bedroom.

were determined to obtain the land by any means necessary. If the rubber tappers refused to sign away their rights to the land, they were threatened and sometimes killed. The ranchers burned down their shacks, sent gunmen to expel them from the land, and had their animals killed.

By the mid-1970s, virtually all of the rubber tappers who lived along the road to Bolivia had been expelled. Many of them migrated to Bolivia, hoping to continue making a living as rubber tappers because it was the only thing they knew how to do. Others moved to the cities, but since they had no other skills and could not read or write, they faced a life of extreme poverty and hardship there. The indigenous (Indian) groups living in the Amazon were also violently expelled, and some of these groups are nearly extinct today.

Selling the rubber estates to cattle ranchers was no less devastating for the forest itself. The ranchers were using a slash-and-burn method for clearing the forest for pasture. They cut down an area of rain forest and left the remaining vegetation to die. Sometimes, they used herbicides to help kill off the vegetation. Then, the area was burned, clearing it for farmland. Although, at first, the ash left from such fires is very rich in nutrients for the soil, this effect only lasts a few years before it becomes impossible to grow anything on that plot.

A large area deforested by soybean farmers is seen this 2004 image of Terra do Meio, Pará, Brazil.

One of the reasons why slash-and-burn results in infertile soil after a few years is erosion. The roots of the trees in the forest help keep erosion to a minimum. In addition, the tree canopy helps protect the soil from being washed away by the heavy rain that is common in the rain forest. A 2.5-acre (1-hectare) plot of intact rain forest only loses about one ton (907 kg) of soil per year. On a cleared area of rain forest of the same size, 20 to 160 tons of soil (18,144 to 145,150 kg) can be washed away per year due to the heavy and frequent rains in that region. The lack of a tree canopy also contributes to erosion, allowing the heavy rains to wash away soil. When all of the fertile soil is washed away, it becomes very difficult to grow anything on the land.

Each cleared pasture only remains fertile for two to three years, and then the rancher must move on to clear a new area for pasture. Each abandoned plot needs at least 30 years to recover. As a result, more and more forest is cleared to sustain cattle ranching and other large-scale agriculture in the Amazon.

Even if a cleared area is left fallow for enough time for things to grow on it again, it never fully recovers to its former state. The intact rain forest has a heavy canopy of trees that block all but 1 or 2 percent of sunlight from reaching the forest floor. The plants that grow under this canopy depend on this darkness and humidity to live. They simply can't survive in the open sunlight.

At the same time, the sections of fallow land cause other changes throughout the forest. Plants depend on insects to pollinate them and animals to spread their seeds so they can continue to reproduce and grow throughout the forest. Birds, insects, and other animals can't cross through the cleared sections, so the plants don't get pollinated and their seeds aren't spread. As a result, clearing sections of land can lead to extinction of many plants in the forest—and the animals that depend on them for food.

Clearing of the forest can also lead to wide-scale drought in the Amazon. The rain forest produces about half of its rainfall through

*(continues on page 36)*

# THE MAGICAL FOREST

Many rubber tappers believe that the ancient rain forest in which they live has magical properties. Stories about various magical creatures that live in the forest are passed down from generation to generation, as well. These include

- **Mapinguari:** The Mapinguari is thought to be a large ape-like or sloth-like creature that can walk on two legs; some say it resembles a hairy man. It is one of the most feared creatures in the rain forest. Some say it has one eye, a foul smell, and likes to eat people alive. There are many reports of Mapinguari sightings in the Amazon, but so far no one has proven that it exists. If it is a real creature, it may be a giant ground sloth, such as a mylodon, which are thought to be long extinct, or some form of anteater.

Known in the Amazon as Mapinguari, this huge, mythological sloth is believed to weigh more than 600 pounds and stand 6 feet tall.

- **Curupira:** The Curupira is also known as the "little forest half-breed" and originates in the mythologies of the Tupi tribe of Brazil. He is said to look like a young boy with real flames for hair and green teeth, and his feet are turned backwards on his legs. His job is to protect the animals of the forest from human destruction. For example, if a rubber tapper kills an animal to eat it, the Curupira has no problem with him, but if someone hunts for sport or pleasure, the Curupira may lay traps and use his backwards foot prints to confuse the hunter and make him lose his way in the forest—or even beat him with tree branches.
- **Mother of the Rubber Tree:** Also known as Queen of the Forest, she is said to be a beautiful woman whose face is cut up in the same way a rubber tree is cut to extract rubber. She helps single men to increase their production of rubber, but they must agree to never marry. If a man does, she will punish him severely. Some older rubber tappers believed that their only chance of paying off their debt to the boss was with the help of the Mother of the Rubber Tree.

Rubber tappers also believe that many "rubber tapper saints" or angels live throughout the Amazon to protect the forest dwellers. These are also called "miraculous souls." For example, St. John of Guarani is the miraculous soul of a rubber tapper who died in the forest in the Guarani homestead. After he died, another rubber tapper became lost in the forest and wandered onto the Guarani homestead. He vowed to light a pound of candles if he could find his way home. Soon, he found his way home, and he believed that the soul of the dead man had helped guide him there. Today, there is a small chapel at the spot of the Guarani homestead, and many rubber tappers visit to make a vow to St. John of Guarani in exchange for his help.

*(continued from page 33)*

the moisture released into the atmosphere by all the vegetation. Clearing significant chunks of the forest reduces the overall amount of rainfall, which can lead to the remaining trees and vegetation dying off—as well as the animals that depend on them.

Most deforestation occurs during the dry season in the Amazon. This season is sometimes now called the burning season because of all the intentional fires that are set to clear the forest. Rubber tappers estimated that between 1970 and 1975, 180,000 rubber trees and 80,000 Brazil nut trees were destroyed in the Xapuri area, where Chico Mendes was from. That number of trees supported approximately 300 rubber-tapping families. It wasn't just the rubber and nut trees that were destroyed: *all* of the vegetation and wildlife were disappearing. "The greatest feeling of desperation dominated the whole region," recalled Mendes in an interview with journalist Augusta Dwyer. "We had to organize ourselves, and that is how the first movement for the defense of the forest began."

## DEFORESTATION AND CLIMATE CHANGE

The deforestation of the Amazon that began in the 1960s didn't only have an impact on the livelihood of rubber tappers and other rural workers. Scientists and environmentalists believe that the world's rain forests play a crucial role in regulating Earth's climate. Clearing these ancient forests is believed to have a significant impact on global warming, or climate change.

Scientists believe that the human-caused emission of greenhouse gases—carbon dioxide, methane, and nitrous oxide—is the primary cause of climate change. Normally, Earth's atmosphere is extremely thin, which allows some of the sun's infrared radiation to escape back into space. This helps keeps Earth at temperatures compatible with life. However, the large amounts of carbon dioxide that we release into the atmosphere (emissions) by driving gasoline-fueled cars, heating our homes with oil, running factories,

A burned nut tree lies on the parched earth near the Alvorada de Amazonia village in the Amazon on November 28, 2009. Slash-and-burn practices are still used to clear land in the Amazon.

and powering electric plants is causing the atmosphere to thicken, which is trapping heat in Earth's atmosphere and raising its overall temperature, causing dangerous changes in our climate.

The trees of the Amazon, often referred to as "Earth's lungs" absorb a significant proportion of carbon dioxide emissions, locking it into their trunks for centuries. This storage system is known as a carbon "sink." In addition to housing the most diverse and rich ecosystem in the world, the Amazon rain forest also represents the world's largest store of carbon.

Carbon sinks are a crucial part of slowing down climate change. Scientists calculate that while humans emit about 32 billion tons (290 million metric tons) of carbon dioxide each year, about half of that is absorbed by natural carbon sinks. This is helping to offset some of the carbon emissions and slow the progress of climate change. The Amazon and other rain forests are considered essential for sustaining life on Earth.

Since large-scale deforestation was initiated in the 1960s, 17 percent of the Amazon rain forest has been destroyed. The impact on

## THE BRAZILIAN BEEF INDUSTRY

Cattle ranching to produce beef still drives much of the deforestation in the Amazon today. In the 1970s and 1980s, Brazil only produced enough beef to feed its own people, but since that time, the beef industry has exploded in Brazil, making the country one of the biggest exporters of beef worldwide. According to Greenpeace United Kingdom (UK), 80 percent of the deforested areas in Brazil are used for cattle ranching today. Its biggest customers are Russia, Egypt, Chile, and the United Kingdom. Some estimates predict that if cattle ranching continues to expand in the Amazon, two-fifths of the world's remaining rain forest will be destroyed.

the local climate is already apparent with increasing droughts taking place in the region. In 2005, the Amazon experienced a devastating drought. Scientists found that during the drought, instead of acting as a carbon sink, the forest actually began emitting carbon dioxide into the atmosphere at an alarming rate. Fortunately, the effect was temporary, but scientists such as Professor Oliver Phillips from the University of Leeds, who was part of the team that studied the carbon emissions in the forest during the drought, warn that "it wouldn't take a huge change to shut down this thing and switch it to an overall source of carbon dioxide."

Yet it is not just the loss of trees in the Amazon that is contributing to climate change. The burning of the forest itself releases significant amounts of greenhouse gases into the atmosphere. As author and Nobel Prize winner Al Gore notes in his 2006 book *An Inconvenient Truth*, close to 30 percent of the world's annual carbon dioxide emissions come from burning of brush land for agriculture and wood fires used for cooking. Once the forest is cleared, large-scale cattle ranching is a significant source of greenhouse gas emissions, as well. Large-scale livestock farms store liquid manure in large tanks, which emit methane—a greenhouse gas.

According to Greenpeace UK, Brazil is now the fourth largest carbon dioxide emitter in the world, and this ranking is largely due to replacing a significant portion of the carbon-storing rain forest with carbon-emitting livestock farms.

## A WORKER'S MOVEMENT IS BORN

The rubber tappers and other rural workers in the Amazon did not know about the global environmental disaster deforestation could cause. What they did know was that the cattle ranchers were robbing them of their livelihood. Living deep in the forest, harvesting rubber and nuts from the trees, was the only life the rubber tappers had ever known. Although it was a life of many hardships, especially under the estate system, the rubber tappers knew that being forced to the cities to live in slums would be far worse. As the old rubber-estate system began to collapse, rubber tappers began to organize and claim their rights to live and work in the forest. A decades-long struggle began between the cattle ranchers and the rubber tappers. Chico Mendes was right in the thick of it.

# Organizing the Rubber Tappers

As the struggle for the rain forest was getting underway, Chico Mendes was ready to play a key role. In their long conversations deep in the forest, Euclides Távora had raised Mendes's awareness of how unfairly the rubber tappers were treated. He predicted that eventually the rural workers would organize a union and encouraged Mendes to get involved when that happened. Mendes always remembered that advice.

In 1968, just three years after he had lost touch with Távora, Mendes tried to organize the rubber tappers, but he was unsuccessful. In the book *Fight for the Forest,* Mendes said that the time simply wasn't right yet. "It was during the hardest years of the dictatorship, and it was very difficult to get people interested," he recalled. He was trying to organize on his own and was unable to get enough support.

Mendes then went to work for the Brazilian Literacy Movement (MOBRAL), a federal program sponsored by the government to address the huge problem of adult illiteracy in Brazil. Until then, he had only been able to apply Távora's teachings to his own experience because he still lived largely in isolation from other rubber tappers. As a literacy teacher, he worked with many rubber tappers and other rural workers, and learned even more about how the rubber tappers

## INDIANS IN THE AMAZON

Rubber tappers were not the only people living in the rain forest. Long before the "soldiers of rubber" were brought to the forest to harvest rubber for the estate owners, many groups of native people (Indians) lived there. In Acre, for example, there are at least 15 indigenous groups. Almost all of these groups have had contact with nonnative society, thanks to the rubber trade and, later, cattle ranching and farming. A few groups, however, have never had contact with Western society.

Native Amazonians survive in the forest using subsistence farming, hunting, and collecting nuts and latex. They clear land for farming using a similar slash-and-burn method described in Chapter 3, but they allow the forest time to recover between plantings, so it does not permanently damage the forest. They cut down trees to clear areas for farming and building their homes out of wood and leaves. They feed their cooking fires with the trees, and use the ashes to return nutrients to the soil. After a few harvests, they move on, allowing the forest to recover, a process that takes about 50 years.

The settlement of the Amazon by rubber-estate owners and others created many problems for the Indians. The first rubber-estate owners rounded them up and forced them to tap rubber for them. With the arrival of the cattle ranchers in the 1970s, many Indians were expelled from their homes in the same way that rubber tappers were. Deforestation has limited the amount of land available to the Indians, which has forced them to return to previously farmed plots of land before they have fully recovered. The Indians are also especially vulnerable to diseases brought to the forest by nonnative were being exploited. It was also during this time that the cattle ranchers began buying up the rubber estates, evicting the rubber tappers, and clearing the forest.

people. Since the disease germs are new to them, they have no immunity, fall sick easily, and have a harder time getting better.

Originally, the rubber tappers that were brought to the forest from other parts of Brazil had a troubled relationship with the Indians. This is mainly because the estate owners would force the rubber tappers to round up the Indians to work on the estates. Later, both groups realized they were victims of the same enemy and joined forces in the fight against deforestation. In the mid-1980s, the Union of Indigenous Nations joined forces with the rubber tappers to form the Alliance of Forest Peoples, ending decades of animosity between rubber tappers and Indians.

In this 1999 image, Yanomami Indians eat plantains while resting in the rain forest.

## EARLY RESISTANCE AND THE *EMPATES*

Although the rubber estates were failing, the rubber tappers were maintaining their small homesteads on the former estates and earning their livelihood by extracting rubber from trees and selling it to small traders and merchants. However, thousands of them were losing their homesteads to the new landowners, who wanted to clear the forest for cattle ranching.

As previously noted, it was relatively easy for the cattle ranchers to expel the rubber tappers. Isolated and illiterate, individual rubber tappers and families had no legal or physical means to fight the ranchers. They were considered squatters and the local judicial system was not sympathetic to them. Furthermore, the ranchers hired gunmen to violently force the rubber tappers off the land. On their own, the rubber tappers had virtually no means to fight these brutal evictions.

As they watched more and more families being forced off the land and into the city slums, the remaining rubber tappers soon realized that they needed to work together to resist the cattle ranchers. At first, they resisted on a grassroots level with the support of the Catholic Church. Later, trade unions were formed to organize the workers so they could speak with one voice, demanding better working conditions and fairer treatment.

The rubber tappers developed a new method of resistance, called an *empate*, or "standoff." The first *empate* occurred in 1973 in the village of Brasiléia. When a new landowner arrived to clear the forest and began trying to expel rubber tappers from the small plots of land they had worked for generations, the rubber tappers would send word to their neighbors. Dozens of rubber tappers and their families would gather at the location where the clear-cutting was about to take place. They would surround the workers just as they were beginning the process of clearing the forest and try to convince them to stop their work. The rubber tappers often carried rifles, but never used them. Because the tree cutters were themselves mostly former rubber tappers, it was usually easy to convince them to stop cutting down the forest. The rubber tappers would force the manager to sign a paper suspending work, and then they would dismantle the camps set up by the workers.

Usually, however, this resulted only in a temporary victory. The landowner would go to the local judge, who was almost always sympathetic to the landowners. The judge would allow deforestation to continue and send police to the site to protect the workers. Still, the rubber tappers refused to give up, and as the rubber tappers—and the *empates* themselves—became better organized, they became more effective in slowing down and stopping deforestation.

The *empates* were a unique tactic of protest invented by the rubber tappers themselves. According to Gomercindo Rodrigues in his book *Walking the Forest with Chico Mendes,* "There is no evidence that any other organization had developed them before." The *empates* became the primary tactic the rubber tappers used to stop deforestation. Hundreds of *empates* have been carried out since the first one in 1973, and the strategy is still used today in the rain forests of Brazil.

## THE RURAL WORKERS' UNIONS

When the rubber tappers first began to organize, they did it on a grassroots level, mostly through the support of Catholic Church communities. Eventually, the movement became a workers' movement. By the mid-1970s, the federal government–backed Agricultural Workers Confederation (CONTAG) was working to establish a rural workers' union in the village of Brasiléia, near Xapuri.

In 1975, Mendes heard about a union training course being offered in Brasiléia. He remembered Távora's advice and enrolled in course right away. He went on to help establish the first rural workers' union in Acre. Mendes served as secretary of that union until 1977. Because he and the other union officers were not paid, they took turns staffing the union office for two or three days at a time while the others worked.

## TRADE UNIONS IN BRAZIL

The trade union system that Chico Mendes entered in 1975 was first established in Brazil in the 1940s under the dictatorship of Getúlio Vargas. Under this system, trade unions operated under the supervision of the Brazilian Ministry of Labor. Unions were divided according to profession and location, and unions of different labor categories were not allowed to collaborate with one another. The government controlled the finances of the union, collecting all dues and distributing funds, and union membership was required. This system limited the true power of the unions to represent workers, since they were under the control of the government. Nevertheless, Mendes still believed that the establishment of the rural workers' unions was a positive step.

In Brasiléia, establishing a union was made easier with the support of the local Catholic bishop, Dom Giocondo. Bishop Giocondo supported the rubber tappers and the union. Many of the union training sessions were held on church premises. Brazil is predominantly Catholic, and, although the law separates church and state, the Catholic Church has a powerful influence. Therefore, the support of the local church leadership was helpful.

## ENTERING PARTY POLITICS

While Mendes was working for the union in Brasiléa, general elections were called in Brazil. The country was still under a military dictatorship, and only two political parties were permitted: the National Renovating Alliance (ARENA) and the Brazilian Democratic Movement (MDB). Although the MDB was really created by the dictatorship to make the government appear more democratic, it became known as the opposition party in Brazil. Mendes was asked to run for a position on the Xapuri city council for the MDB party. He agreed, thinking that he would just be a name on the ballot without much chance of winning. Much to his surprise, he won the election.

The newly elected city council had three MDB members and four ARENA members. As the party of the military regime, ARENA was on the side of the landowners. Although the MDB was technically the opposition party, Mendes quickly learned that he would not find much support for the rubber tappers among his party colleagues.

Finding himself thrust into party politics with little experience was difficult for Mendes. "My background was in the trade union movement, but now I had to get on with both the political party and the trade union aspects of the struggle," he recalled in his autobiography. He tried to push initiatives to stop the ranchers from evicting the rubber tappers from their land, but even his fellow MDB party members did not support him. He began receiving death threats and was almost expelled from the party because of his attempts to expose the violence that the rubber tappers were enduring.

Despite his disappointment in the political system, Mendes persevered, and even served as president of the city council for a brief period in 1979. As president, he made an angry speech to the council in which he berated politicians for ignoring the plight of the rubber tappers. "There is no hope for the rubber tappers, and injustices are constantly noted," he said.

As city council president, he also organized a meeting between city council members and the rubber tappers to discuss the deforestation, violence, and exploitation that the rubber tappers faced. After this meeting, some of the council members from his own party tried to get him kicked off the council. He gave up the presidency in order to keep his seat, and remained on the city council until 1983. Throughout his time on the council, Mendes continued to speak out on behalf of the rubber tappers and denounce the devastation of the rain forest being carried out by the new landowners with the help of the police. Pushing for protection of the rain forest was an unusual stance during this period, but Mendes was ahead of his time in many ways.

In 1977, Mendes decided the time was right to return to Xapuri and establish a union there. At first, the union organizers faced more local opposition than they had in Brasiléia. One reason was that, in Xapuri, the union leaders did not enjoy the same support from the local Catholic leadership that they had in Brasiléia. José Carneiro de Lima, an influential local priest, had close ties with the landowners and tried to stop the workers from organizing in any way. When he learned that Chico Mendes was trying to organize a union, he reported him to the local police, who took Mendes in for questioning.

That was the first of many encounters with Brazil's legal system for Mendes. Under the dictatorship, anyone who opposed the government's agenda was considered an enemy, and by fighting the deforestation project, Mendes was fighting the government's agenda of developing the Amazon. This put him at odds with the powerful landowners, the police who were primarily there to support the government and protect the landowners, and the government itself. It took a tremendous amount of courage and commitment on the part of Mendes and his fellow union organizers to speak out against deforestation and fight for the rights of the rubber tappers.

For the next several years, Mendes juggled his roles as union organizer, city council member, and rubber tapper. He played an active role in establishing the union in Xapuri, but he was not allowed to be an official union leader while he was still in public office on the city council. He was also required to work as a rubber tapper in order to join the union, so he went into the forest to harvest rubber and Brazil nuts when the council was not in session. Mendes recalled these years as being very challenging for him.

Eventually, the conservative priest, José Carneiro de Lima, left the area, and the union began to enjoy more support from the Church. Mendes continued to play an active role in the union's decision making even though he wasn't an official union leader at the time.

## VIOLENCE INTENSIFIES

As the unions in Brasiléia and Xapuri became stronger, tensions between the rubber tappers and the landowners increased. In 1977, after Mendes went to Xapuri to help establish the union there, Wilson Pinheiro was elected president of the union in Brasiléia. "He was a very able and courageous person who strengthened the movement a lot," recalled Mendes in *Fight for the Forest.*

In 1979, Pinheiro organized a large *empate* in Boco do Acre, in the state of Amazonas. More than 300 rubber tappers went with Pinheiro to drive out a group of gunmen who were trying to force the people off the land. The *empate* was successful. Although they carried only knives and sickles, the rubber tappers managed to disarm the gunmen, collecting more than 20 automatic rifles, and drive them off the land.

The success of Pinheiro's *empate* worried the landowners. They began to realize that the rubber tappers' organized resistance was a real threat to their efforts to clear the ancient forest for cattle ranching and farming. To stop the resistance movement, they planned to kill Wilson Pinheiro and a leader from Xapuri. "That could easily have been me," recalled Mendes. They hired two gunmen, and, on July 21, 1980, one of the gunmen walked into the Brasiléia Rural Workers' union office and shot Pinheiro, killing him. The other gunman went to Xapuri, but the leaders of the Xapuri union were at a meeting in another area, and he failed to find anyone on his list. Many believed that Chico Mendes was the second gunman's target.

Angry about Pinheiro's death, the rubber tappers gave the police seven days to take action in the investigation of his murder. In response, the police, as always on the side of the landowners, did very little. On the seventh day, the rubber tappers held a memorial service for Pinheiro. On the same day, a ranch manager who was believed to have participated in the plot to kill Pinheiro was himself killed. The rubber tappers were blamed, but many say that the ranchers had him killed in order to blame it on the rubber tappers and divert the police's attention from Pinheiro's murder.

Chico Mendes stands outside the headquarters of the rubber tappers union in Xapuri in December 1988.

Although the police had not taken aggressive action to find Pinheiro's killers, they acted quickly when the ranch manager was killed. They immediately began rounding up hundreds of rubber tappers, who were arrested and interrogated. Some were even tortured and reported having their nails torn out with pliers. Chico Mendes was among those arrested and indicted. He and others were put on trial in military court for inciting violence against the ranch manager. They were acquitted. Later, 17 rural workers were put on trial for killing the ranch manager, but they were found not guilty based on evidence that the workers were framed by the ranchers. No one was ever arrested or charged with the murder of Pinheiro.

## LESSONS LEARNED

The repression that resulted following Pinheiro's murder was a blow to the resistance movement in Brasiléia, but the workers were not ready to give up. Resistance to deforestation continued, with Xapuri as the new base for organizing the rural workers. Mendes and the other leaders in Xapuri had learned some lessons from what had happened in Brasiléia.

Because the leadership in Brasiléia had been so centralized, it was difficult for the movement to recover after Pinheiro's death and the repression that followed. In Xapuri, Mendes and the other leaders decided to take steps to prevent this from happening again. After the Pinheiro incident, Mendes talked with one of the other Xapuri union leaders. They agreed to spend most of their time working in different areas. "We must separate now because some day our enemies will catch up with us and kill us both," Mendes told his colleague. "But if we separate and they kill you, I will keep trying to build a movement and if they kill me, you keep doing the same."

The Xapuri union also took a more grassroots approach to organizing. They encouraged the workers to be far more involved in planning the resistance. They worked to create a movement that was strong throughout its base, rather than being dependent on a few central leaders to keep it going.

# Lighting the Way: Educating the Rubber Tappers

When the central activity of the rural workers' movement shifted to Xapuri, Chico Mendes was still on the Xapuri city council. For a short time, the Xapuri union was lead by a woman named Derci Teles de Carvalho. By 1981, Mendes had left office and was elected president of the Xapuri Rural Workers' Union. During this time, the rubber tappers' movement had not only shifted its location from Brasiléia to Xapuri, it had shifted its focus, too.

## THE RUBBER TAPPER PROJECT (*PROJETO SERINGUERO*)

The *empates* continued in Xapuri, but the union leaders knew that more was needed to strengthen the movement against deforestation. The union began to broaden its focus from the immediate need to stop the ranchers from expelling workers from their land to improving the living conditions of the rubber tappers. They hoped that better living conditions would strengthen the rubber tappers' motivation to remain in the forest and fight the landowners. With this goal in mind, the Rubber Tapper Project (*Projeto Seringuero*) was established to develop schools and cooperatives for the rural workers.

## Schools

Many rural workers could not read or write, and this made it difficult for them to understand their troubling situation. Because they had been exploited and powerless for so long, they simply did not believe they could fight the landowners. The union hoped that by offering literacy classes they would attract more people to the movement and increase the rubber tappers' understanding of what was being done to them, why it was wrong, and what could be done to stop it. The education program aimed to not only teach people how to read and

Students work at their desks in a school founded by Chico Mendes in Cachoeira village. Students there, members of rubber-tapper families, range in age from 3 to 60.

# THE CATHOLIC CHURCH AND THE RUBBER TAPPERS' MOVEMENT

Brazil boasts the largest Catholic congregation in the world. Until 1889, Catholicism was the official religion of Brazil, but since that time, the country has established the policy of separation of church and state. Even so, Catholicism has remained the predominant religion in the country.

Under the military dictatorship, the Catholic Church was the only group that was permitted to work openly to help the poor. During the 1970s and 1980s, the Church established thousands of grassroots church communities to promote religious teaching as well as social action. These congregations were taught that the current social structure was not the will of God, and they were encouraged to work for radical change to create a society that was more in line with Christian values. However, in some parts of the country, the Church is more conservative.

As mentioned, the relationship between the local Church and the rubber tappers' movement has been mixed. In Brasiléia, the Church community was quite progressive and gave the union a lot of support. In Xapuri, the union was at first at odds with the Church, thanks to one conservative priest, but eventually, relations between the union and the Church improved. The Church's national Pastoral Land Commission later became involved in the rubber tappers' movement. In addition, the Catholic Church provided funding for the Ecumenical Documentation and Information Center, which worked closely with the Rubber Tappers' Project to establish education programs. Although the relationship was not without its struggles, Mendes viewed the Church as an ally in the rubber tappers' struggle.

write, but also "to learn more about [the forest itself] and defend it," according to Mendes.

The union began working to establish the first schools in 1979, and, by 1982, the education program was gaining momentum. The literacy programs were developed by the Ecumenical Documentation and Information Center (CEDI), funded by Oxfam International and later the Ecumenical Services Network. Eventually, the Brazilian government began to help cover some of the costs of running the schools. "Things went slowly, but, even so, the program began to make a big contribution by getting rubber tappers to think more about what was going on around them," recalled Mendes in *Fight for the Forest.*

Initially, the literacy program focused on adults. People were selected by their communities to receive training and improve their literacy skills. Once they had completed the training, they returned to their own communities to set up local literacy classes. By 1988, there were 18 schools in the Xapuri area.

Those who wanted to attend the new schools also had to continue working to support their families, so the classes had to be structured in a way to avoid taking too much of the students' time. Classes were held on weekends. Students could continue to work during the week, and spend the weekends at school—just as Chico Mendes had spent his weekends studying with Euclides Távora and his weekdays tapping rubber to help support his family.

The spread of literacy among the rubber tappers made organizing the union much easier. In addition to reading and writing skills, the ideas behind the union were also spread throughout the forest. Many of the students in the schools became union representatives. On a practical level, increased literacy made it easier to communicate and spread information about union activities.

Although the schools initially focused on adults, many of the rubber tappers began to ask for schools to be set up for their children. They felt it was more important for their children to learn to read and write. Eventually, organizers developed schools for children, as well. This has resulted in the education of a whole new generation

## LITERACY IN BRAZIL TODAY

Despite the efforts of the Rubber Tappers' Project, adult literacy—and education in general—remains a significant problem in Brazil today. According to 2006 statistics, 14.6 million people, ages 15 and above, are completely illiterate. Thirty-three million Brazilians are functionally illiterate—meaning they can read and write simple sentences, but do not have the literacy skills to function in daily life. They cannot read material such as employment advertisements, newspaper articles, bills, bank paperwork, instructions, road signs, and other forms of writing. The illiteracy rate is highest in the rural parts of Brazil and lowest in the urban areas, where it is more comparable to the rate in industrialized nations.

In 2003, President Luiz Inácio Lula da Silva (known popularly as "Lula") made literacy a political priority and for the first time in Brazil's history, education was recognized as a fundamental right for all citizens. Programs were put in place to improve access to education for the rural poor. In 2003, President Lula launched the Literate Brazil program which trains literacy teachers and provides literacy education for youth and adults, ages 15 and above. Since that time, the program has provided literacy education to at least 8 million people, but Brazil still has a long way to go in addressing the literacy rates among its poor rural population.

of rubber tappers who work to protect the forest. "They learn about our *empates* at school and often insist on taking part themselves!" Mendes said in an interview.

## The Cooperatives

Another component of the Rubber Tappers' Project involved setting up cooperatives. As the debt-bondage system of the traditional rubber estate began to break down, the rubber tappers' only choice was to sell their rubber to individual traders who came through the forest to buy rubber and sell basic goods such as sugar and other staples. As they did with the rubber estates, these traders offered unfairly low prices for rubber while selling their own goods at inflated prices. Since the rubber tappers had no means to transport their harvests to towns where they could get a fairer price, their only choice was to sell to these traders.

The Rubber Tappers' Project first introduced the idea of cooperatives in the early 1980s. Three cooperatives were formed to test the idea. Each cooperative was made of rubber tappers who lived near one another in the forest. They were provided with initial funding from Oxfam to purchase mules or boats to transport their collective harvests to the nearest town, where they were able to receive a fair price for the goods.

Getting the rubber tappers to work together proved challenging. As mentioned, the rubber estate owners purposely kept the rubber tappers isolated from one another. They also enlisted certain rubber tappers to spy on other tappers and report to the boss when anyone tried to sell their rubber off the estate. This fostered a deep sense of mistrust among the rubber tappers. In addition, the rubber tappers saw the cooperatives as an "outsiders" notion—one that was introduced by the leaders of the Rubber Tappers' Project and not by the rubber tappers themselves. The first attempts to establish cooperatives were unsuccessful.

In 1987, the union tried again, this time holding meetings throughout Xapuri to discuss the idea of cooperatives with the rubber tappers. The members still faced resistance, but this time they were able to overcome opposition and, in 1988, the Agro-extractive Cooperative of Xapuri, Ltd. was established. At first, only 33 members joined, but once people saw that the cooperative was successfully allowing members to market rubber for better prices than they would get individually, the cooperative grew to be 300 strong. It still exists today.

## Health Posts

As head of the Xapuri Rural Workers' Union, Mendes also led the way in improving the health care available to the rubber tappers. Before this initiative, rural workers had very little access to medical care and supplies. In 1985, the union worked with State Health Secretary Zé Alberto to build six health clinics to serve rubber tappers and their families. Members of the community were also selected to become "health promoters." They were provided with basic health care training and provided health and nutrition education, as well as first aid in their communities.

Unfortunately, the government eventually withdrew support for the health centers. The health promoters continued their work on a volunteer basis, but finding financial support to keep the clinics staffed and stocked with medical supplies became challenging. Today, rubber tappers still have difficulty accessing needed health care and supplies.

## MARRIAGE AND FAMILY

Mendes's devotion to the cause of the rubber tappers did not mean he had no personal life. In 1968, Mendes married Maria Eunice Feitosa. Although their marriage did not last long and they lived in extreme poverty, they had two daughters: Angela, who was born a little more than a year after they were married, and Roseangela. The couple separated before Roseangela's birth, and she died at 11 months old, before ever meeting her father.

In 1983, Mendes married Ilzamar "Ilza" G. Bezzera. He had known Ilza since she was a child living on the Santa Fe rubber estate. Mendes tapped rubber there and befriended Ilza's father, Jose Moacir Gadelha. When Ilza was 17, she and Mendes fell in love and were married a short time later.

Life as a married couple was far from easy for the Mendeses. Mendes had no money since he didn't earn a salary from the union, and so they lived with friends in Xapuri for about a year. In 1984,

Chico Mendes poses at home with his wife Ilza, son Sandino, and daughter Elenira in 1988.

Mendes and Ilza had their first child together, a daughter named Elenira. After this, they went to live with Ilza's family on the Santa Fe estate. Mendes travelled a lot for his work for the union but returned home as often as he could. In 1986, Ilza almost died giving birth to twins, only one of whom survived. They named him Sandino. Both children were named after famous revolutionaries.

In the face of many challenges, Mendes continued to lead the rubber tappers in their fight for the rain forest. The Rubber Tappers' Project helped improve the living conditions of many rubber tappers, and it helped to build community among them and spread the word about the work the union was doing to protect the rubber tappers and the forest. The movement began to gain momentum.

## 6

# Bringing the Cause to the World

The work of the Rubber Tappers' Project progressed, and the *empates* continued. Meanwhile, the government continued its push to clear the forest to make way for economic development. It seemed that in addition to the standoffs taking place on individual estates, the two sides of the struggle were at a standoff on a larger scale throughout Brazil, as well. On one side were Brazilian politicians and business people. They weren't concerned about the welfare of the rubber tappers, and they didn't appreciate the ecological importance of the rain forest. They wanted to make money and develop Brazil's economy and felt that clearing the rain forest for ranching and farming was the way to do it. On the other side were the rubber tappers and other rural workers. They simply wanted the right to remain in the forest and earn their living the way they always had.

Would this standoff ever end? Chico Mendes and his supporters began to realize that if they were going to make progress against deforestation, they needed to propose an alternative plan for developing the rain forest economically while leaving it largely intact.

The union began to discuss ways to bring rubber tappers together to discuss alternatives and to make their cause more visible to the world beyond the rain forest.

There was a third group that had a stake in the fate of the rain forest, but they hadn't entered into the struggle just yet. These were the environmentalists. Since deforestation had begun in the 1970s, environmental groups such as the U.S.–based Environmental Defense Fund had been concerned about the destruction of the ancient forests and what it might mean for the planet. Radical environmentalists wanted the rain forest left alone completely, but most accepted that the forest was not only important ecologically, but that it also represented vast natural resources that could help people economically.

## THE FIRST NATIONAL RUBBER TAPPERS' CONGRESS

Mendes and his comrades in Xapuri decided to plan a national meeting of rubber tappers to discuss how the movement might move forward. Holding such a meeting would cost money, so, in May 1985, Mendes went to Brasiléia to work with his friend Mary Allegretti in seeking financial support for the meeting. The National Heritage Department of the Ministry of Culture, Oxfam, and other groups agreed to support the meeting.

Mendes returned to Xapuri and began making plans for the meeting, which was scheduled for October 1985 in Brasiléia. Bringing together rubber tappers from the whole Amazon region to travel to the meeting was not a simple task. Remember, rubber tappers did not have telephones or cars—let alone computers, e-mail, and the Internet. Mendes established an organizing committee with representatives from the Rural Workers' Union, the Rubber Tappers' Project, and other organizations. Some of these representatives traveled to different parts of the Amazon to spread the word about the meeting.

In October, more than 100 rubber tappers travelled to the University of Brasiléia for the first National Rubber Tappers' Congress. They came from the Brazilian states of Acre, Amazonas, and

Rondonia and represented 17 different rural workers' unions and rubber tappers' organizations. For many of them, this was their first time leaving home. They travelled for days on foot, by boat, and by bus to get to the meeting.

The congress, which lasted a week, included meetings with officials from various government departments who sympathized with

## MARY HELENA ALLEGRETTI

One of Mendes's close friends and advisors, Mary Allegretti, is an anthropologist who studied at the University of Brasiléia. She completed field research in the Amazon, and, in 1979, wrote a thesis about the traditional rubber estates in Acre. She helped the Rubber Tappers' Project establish the literacy education and cooperatives in Xapuri in the early 1980s. In 1984, she joined a human rights organization in Brasiléia and began to lobby the government in support of the rubber tappers. She helped Chico Mendes obtain support for the first National Rubber Tappers' Congress in 1985 and was one of the people who conceived the plan for extractive reserves in the Amazon.

Allegretti went on to devote her life to advocating for the Amazon and the rubber tappers. She served as state secretary of environment, science, and technology for the Brazilian state of Amapá, and later became national secretary for the Amazon region at the Brazilian Ministry for the Environment. For her work advocating for the rubber tappers and environmental policy in Brazil, Allegretti has won several awards, including the United Nations Environment Programme (UNEP) Global 500 prize in 1990 and the World Wildlife Federation's Duke of Edinburgh Conservation Medal in 1991. She continues to speak around the world, advocating for sustainable development of the Amazon.

the rubber tappers. Also in attendance was Dr. Stephen Schwartz-man of the Environmental Defense Fund. Dr. Schwartzman educated Mendes and the other attendees about the international environmental movement and the global importance of preserving the rain forests.

At the end of the congress, the attendants produced a document listing 63 demands regarding the development of the Amazon, covering land reform, rubber policy, nutrition, health and education, and even pensions and social security for rubber tappers. The first two demands were as follows:

> We demand a developmental policy for Amazonia that meets the interests of rubber tappers and respects our rights. We do not accept an Amazon development policy that favors large enterprises which exploit and massacre rural workers and destroy nature.
>
> We are not opposed to technology, provided that it is at our service and does not ignore our wisdom, our experience, our interests and our rights.

The second paragraph shows that the rubber tappers were not opposed to economic development in the rain forest. Rather, they demanded that any development should be done in a way that respects the forest and the rights of those who live there.

Another important outcome of the meeting was the formation of the National Rubber Tappers' Council (CNS). Whereas the rural workers' unions represented the interests of many other types of rural workers in addition to rubber tappers, the CNS focused on the specific interests of rubber tappers. It was formed to counter the National Rubber Council, which represented the interests of landowners and businessmen. The CNS quickly worked to ally itself with other rural groups, forming the Alliance of Forest Peoples with the Union of Indigenous Nations. Mendes became the primary spokesperson for both the CNS and the Alliance of Forest Peoples.

## FINDING COMMON GROUND:
## THE EXTRACTIVE RESERVES

The most important outcome of the first National Rubber Tappers' Congress was the proposal for establishing extractive reserves throughout the Amazon. The extractive reserves would be large, demarcated, publicly owned areas within the forest. Rubber tappers and other traditional groups would maintain the right to live and work in the reserves, as long as they did not destroy the forest. The rubber tappers, Brazil-nut harvesters, and others could live in these areas and continue to earn their living as they always had without fear of being expelled by ranchers or other landowners. The communities in the reserves would determine their own basic rules, but no one could destroy the forest.

The extractive-reserve concept was a significant breakthrough in the struggle against deforestation because it addressed the interests of all three of the major stakeholders: rubber tappers, who wanted to continue their way of life in the forest; environmentalists, who were concerned about the global impact of developing forest land for ranching and farming; *and* the government, which wanted to find ways to use the forest land for economic development. This concept was a model for *sustainable* development—a way to take advantage of the forest economically without destroying it. It was the alternative plan that the rubber tappers needed to counter the government's argument that the country needed to clear the forest for economic development.

The extractive-reserve concept was not just intended for rubber tappers. Mendes and other promoters of this idea hoped to encourage extracting and marketing of all kinds of natural resources in the forest, from rubber to nuts to medicinal plants, and even fishing. They believed that the region had potential to play an important role in Brazil's economy if left intact.

The idea caught on. A working group was established to explore the extractive-reserve idea further. Mendes worked closely with Dr. Schwartzman to research and advocate for the extractive-reserves idea.

In the meantime, the political climate in Brazil was shifting. In 1985, the military regime that had reigned in Brazil since 1964 finally came to an end. The new civilian government introduced a land-reform law, the National Plan for Agrarian Reform, which, among other things, allowed for setting aside public land for the rubber tappers to make their living on without destroying the forest. For the first time, it seemed as though the government was going to support the cause of the rubber tappers. In response, however, the powerful ranchers and developers lobbied politicians intensely, and by the time the law was passed, it favored the landowners more than the rural workers. The law still allowed for the extractive reserves in theory, but it made it much more difficult to actually set aside land.

Meanwhile, tensions continued to rise between the ranchers and the rural workers. The ranchers were determined to hold onto their property and fight the extractive reserves. To that end, they organized their own group, called the Democratic Ruralist Union (UDR). While the UDR claimed to be a democratic organization with the aim of defending their rights to own private property and to practice free enterprise, the organization's real primary activity was amassing weapons and developing private militia groups. In 1987, one of the group's leaders, Salvador Farina, admitted that the group had amassed more than 70,000 weapons—one for every member.

As both the UDR and the rubber tappers' movement grew in strength, conflicts over land continued to intensify. In Acre, the UDR had strong support among local politicians and judges. Every time an *empate* succeeded in temporarily stopping a clear-cut operation, the ranchers went to court to ask for police protection so they could continue deforestation. Since the judges were still generally sympathetic to the ranchers, they often won.

The UDR also began strategically killing union leaders and other prominent supporters of the rural workers' movement, such as priests, lawyers, and advisers. These retaliations caused major setbacks to the movement's activities and made its work more difficult. In most cases, no one was ever arrested for these crimes.

## INTERNATIONAL ATTENTION

Despite the setbacks caused by the UDR and the disappointing land-reform law passed in 1985, Mendes continued to push for the extractive reserves to be established. He became the primary spokesperson promoting the idea of extractive reserves, and the rubber tappers' cause began to receive international attention from environmental groups, especially in the United States. This marked a turning point in the fight for the rain forest, merging what had been purely a workers' movement with a global environmental cause.

In 1987, the EDF and the National Wildlife Federation invited Mendes to the United States to represent the CNS at the annual board meeting of the Inter-American Development Bank (IDB). IDB had provided Brazil a loan for the completion of a road project in Acre. The Brazilian government had been building roads through the Amazon to allow for settlement and development, and with these roads came environmental destruction and human disaster. Mendes wanted to avoid such a disaster with the road project in Acre. He went to the meeting hoping to convince the IDB to demand that Brazil complete this project in a more environmentally responsible manner.

Mendes spoke no English at all and had no money with him when he stepped off the plane in Miami, Florida. The fact that he had no money made customs officials suspicious: What was someone who didn't carry any money doing in the United States? Mendes was almost sent back to Brazil, but when he finally showed the officials an invitation to the IDB meeting from Dr. Schwartzman, they realized that he had a legitimate reason for entering the country and let him go.

Even so, Mendes would not have been allowed to attend the meeting simply as a rubber tapper, even with his invitation from the EDF. To gain entry, he also needed to obtain a press pass from a television station in London. While at the meeting, members of environmental organizations introduced Mendes to various board members of the IDB to whom he made his case for the Amazon.

Chico Mendes stands among earth-digging machines on BR 364, a road he protested against.

Mendes also travelled to Washington, D.C., where he met with staff members of the U.S. Senate Budget Committee. In a series of meetings and interviews, Mendes made his case for establishment of the extractive reserves to protect the Amazon. He also criticized multilateral banks for providing funding for the building of roads through the Amazon—roads which had lead to environmental and human disaster.

His travels were worth the effort. In the end, the IDB suspended the loan for the road project and, with Mendes's input, renegotiated the loan terms to ensure that Brazil would protect the environment and the traditional populations that could be affected by the road as much as possible. Mendes returned to Brazil with an agreement between the IDB and Brazil for paving the road in Acre that included $10 million for protecting the environment and the traditional populations that lived along the road.

Back home in Acre, Mendes was sharply criticized for his work at the IDB meeting. Politicians accused him of trying to block funding for the road project, when, in fact, he had simply been trying to ensure Brazil's compliance with environmental standards before moving forward with the road. Mendes's opponents also tried to make it look as if he had gone for self-serving reasons, accusing him of coming back to Brazil with "pocketfuls of money." In fact, Mendes left Miami as penniless as he had been when he

## UNITED NATIONS HONOR FOR MENDES

The United Nations Environment Programme launched the Global 500 Laureate Roll of Honour in 1987. It was established to recognize individuals and organizations for their achievements in protecting the environment. The Global 500 prize continues to attract widespread media and political attention to environmental causes around the world.

Chico Mendes was among the first 91 activists to be awarded the prize back in 1987. Since the prize was launched, more than 680 individuals and organizations have received the Global 500 Award for Environmental Achievement. Some recipients of the award from the United States include

- Robert Redford (1987)
- National Geographic Society (1987)
- Former president Jimmy Carter (1988)
- Children's Alliance for the Protection of the Environment (1990)
- Jane Goodall (1997)

arrived, with just a few dollars that his friends had given him to cover meals and traveling fees. The increasing international exposure and credibility that Mendes and his cause were receiving made the supporters of the landowners desperate to discredit him in any way they could.

Although Mendes was criticized by politicians at home, his cause was receiving more and more attention outside of Brazil. After his attendance at the IDB meeting, Robert Lamb of the UNEP visited Xapuri. In 1987, UNEP awarded its Global 500 prize to Mendes for his work in protecting the rain forest. Of the award's 91 recipients that year, Mendes was the only Brazilian. Once again, local politicians were outraged—this time, it was because the prize was awarded to a private individual instead of government officials. Mendes received virtually no recognition for the prize at home, but the award brought even more international attention to his cause. He travelled to London to receive the prize, which he dedicated to the rubber tappers of Amazonia.

That same year, Mendes was again recognized for his work by the international community. This time, he was awarded a prize from the Better World Society, which was established by Ted Turner, the founder of cable news channel CNN. Mendes travelled to New York to receive the prize, which he again dedicated to the rubber tappers. In New York, he stayed at the Waldorf Astoria Hotel. He estimated that the money spent on each breakfast at the hotel could have supported a rubber tapper and his family for an entire month.

Mendes faced further criticism when he returned to Brazil. Local and state officials continued to denounce him, accusing him of being a false leader and of trying to damage Brazil's economic development. The state legislature even called him to testify about the reasons for his visits abroad. The more international attention he received, the more uncomfortable local politicians became. They couldn't understand how a simple rubber tapper could be getting so much international recognition.

Mendes responded to the criticism in the same calm and diplomatic manner with which he led his movement. He understood that the politicians were simply desperate to stop the momentum of his

While in New York City to accept his award from the Better World Society, Chico Mendes was given a room at the Waldorf Astoria. He was surprised by the costs associated with staying at the luxurious hotel.

movement in any way they could, even by turning the rural workers against him. He felt this was a sign of the movement's strength. "In a sense I consider this a victory of the workers," he told his friend Gomercindo Rodrigues in an interview published in Rodrigues's 2007 book, *Walking the Forest with Chico Mendes.* "To me it's clear that they are against us and are worried by the situation because they defend the landowners. So it's obvious they feel bad because their interests were being threatened," he continued.

It was this attitude that kept Mendes moving forward in his work on behalf of the rubber tappers. He knew that the more anger he felt from the opposition, the more worried they must be about his movement. He took this to be a sign of his movements' strength, and he refused to be discouraged.

Despite what the politicians said about him, Mendes had nothing to gain personally by leading the rubber tappers' movement. He did not receive a salary from the union. His dedication to the rubber tappers' cause put a great strain on his second (and, likely, his first) marriage in emotional and practical ways. Mendes spent a great deal of time travelling for the union, and he refused to bring his wife, Ilza, with him on these trips. The Mendeses did not even have a house of their own until friends helped them buy one in 1988. Until then, they lived in their parents' homes and relied on support from friends and family to survive so that Mendes could continue leading the struggle.

Nevertheless, Mendes felt these personal sacrifices were worth it. He knew what he was working for was the right thing for the rubber tappers and the rain forest. "If you think only about your private issues, about finances, about personal advantage, you won't succeed in holding onto this idealism or in fighting for the workers," he told Gomercindo Rodrigues. Although many of his colleagues dropped out of the struggle over the years, Mendes maintained his idealism and persevered.

# Progress—and Retaliation

Despite the growing international attention to the rubber tappers' movement, the forest continued to burn. In 1987, a satellite detected large fires along the BR-364, one of the highways built in the 1970s to bring people to the Amazon. Along both sides of the highway, over an area twice the size of Switzerland, more than 200,000 intentional fires were burning. A Brazilian researcher calculated that the fires emitted more than 500 million tons (454 million metric tons) of carbon into the atmosphere—equal to 10 percent of the world's greenhouse gases.

Meanwhile, Chico Mendes continued to travel around Brazil speaking out on behalf of the rubber tappers and advocating for the extractive reserves. He remained based in Xapuri organizing and leading *empates* with the rural workers. The movement was now too loud and too strong to be ignored at home. In June 1988, he visited Rio de Janeiro, where the city council gave him the keys to the city. It was the first time he had been publicly recognized and celebrated in his own country.

The rubber tappers also continued to stage *empates* to stop the ranchers from clearing the forest. These protests continued to be nonviolent despite the fact that their enemies, the cattle ranchers, were now fully armed and "quite happy using violence," as Mendes said in *Fight for the Forest*. In fact, by 1988, the ranchers had begun killing some of the rubber tappers, and it was widely known that they had plans to start going after the movement's leaders, including Mendes. While Mendes worried about the escalating violence and feared that one day the rubber tappers would have to fight back, he remained committed to keeping the rubber tappers' protests nonviolent for as long as possible.

By 1988, the rubber tappers had two additional tools in their arsenal to stop the ranchers. The first was the official establishment of extractive reserves. The government now had the legal means to expropriate, or reassign, land from the ranchers and establish extractive reserves, protecting the rubber tappers' right to stay on the land and protecting the forest itself from destruction. However, the government still tended to support the landowners more than the rural workers. It took a great deal of effort to convince the government to take these steps, but Mendes and the rubber tappers were willing to work tirelessly for their cause.

The other important tool the rubber tappers now had was an audience of supporters. Thanks to the international attention Mendes had brought to the rubber tappers' cause, the media was now paying attention to what was happening in the rain forest. When the rubber tappers organized an *empate*, they also sent a team to Xapuri to make sure the news of the event was relayed throughout Brazil and around the world. This attention put additional pressure on the Brazilian government to support the rubber tappers.

Meanwhile, thanks in part to Mendes's travels overseas and his collaboration with the international environmental movement, the Brazilian government was under increasing pressure from the international community to show that it was protecting the rain forest. For example, politicians from Brazil promised the IDB that they would enact better protections of the forest and place more limits on cattle ranching. In reality, however, the politicians still supported the ranchers and took steps to protect them whenever possible. In any case, the increased awareness of deforestation put additional pressure on the government to give in to the rubber tappers' demands.

## *EMPATES* AT ECUADOR AND CACHOEIRA

Things came to a head on the Ecuador Cachoeira rubber estate in Xapuri in May 1988. In 1987, a portion of the Cachoeira estate was purchased by a rancher named Darli Alves da Silva. He was the head of a brutal ranching family that had arrived in Xapuri in 1974 and began buying up land from the rubber-estate owners and clearing it for pasture. The Alves da Silva family was known to use especially violent means to expel rubber tappers from the land they had acquired. Originally from southeastern Brazil, the family had moved several times in order to escape arrest for murdering rivals over land disputes, until finally ending up in the Amazon. Throughout the 1970s and 1980s, they continued to acquire land from the rubber-estate owners and expand their ranching enterprise.

The Cachoeira estate happened to be the same estate that Chico Mendes grew up on and where he had worked as a rubber tapper for more than 20 years. When Darli Alves da Silva acquired the land, as many as 80 rubber-tapping families had been living there for generations. He began trying to force these families off the land so he could clear it for pasture. Mendes worked hard to convince the families to stay put to protect their homesteads and the forest from Alves da Silva's brutal ways.

To stop Alves da Silva from entering the estate and cutting the forest down, all of the families living on Cachoeira gathered together to guard the entrance of the estate. They also called upon the rubber tappers from several neighboring estates to help. This was a different kind of *empate* because the deforestation of this

Large plots of land were actively being deforested in and near Acre, as this 1987 image shows.

area had not yet begun. This time, the workers wanted to stop the ranchers from entering the estate at all and forcing them to give up their homesteads.

The workers remained camped at the entrance for almost a month. Mendes stayed in the union offices in Xapuri where he gathered information and let people know about the *empate*. Each day, he drove the union's pickup truck to the site to deliver supplies, news, and encouragement to the rubber tappers. They managed to keep Alves da Silva out of the estate for the time being.

However, while the *empate* at the Cachoeira was still going on, another one began brewing at a nearby estate. The Ecuador estate had recently been sold to the Delta Construction Company, which obtained permission from the federal forestry board to clear 123 acres (50 hectares) of forest for cattle pasture.

By this time, several laws had been passed to regulate deforestation. For example, in 1986, a law was put on the books that prohibited cutting down rubber and brazil nut trees. Another law prohibited deforestation of hillsides, which causes soil erosion. Landowners were also required to provide a plan for managing the forest if more than 123 acres (50 hectares) were being cleared. However, these laws were generally ignored. It was widely believed that the cattle ranchers regularly bribed the forestry board to ignore the restrictions.

To try to stop the clear-cut on the Ecuador estate, the Xapuri Rural Workers Union and the CNS immediately filed objections with the forestry board. They claimed that the permission to clear the forest had been granted illegally and that the construction company actually planned to clear as many as 741 acres (300 hectares) of forest. Mendes even visited the governor of Acre to try to convince him to put a stop to the deforestation.

The union received no response to their objections from the forestry board, so they staged an *empate* on the estate to try to stop the clear-cutting from taking place. In response, the ranchers went to court and requested police protection so they could continue the deforestation. As was often the case, the judge sided

# THE NATIONAL ANTHEM OF BRAZIL

The Brazilian National Anthem was composed in the 1800s by Francisco Manual da Silva as a purely instrumental tune to be played by a military band. Later, in 1909, Joaquim Osório Duque Estrada wrote lyrics to go with it. The following version of the translated lyrics was officially adopted as the national anthem in 1922:

I

The peaceful banks of the Ipiranga
Heard the resounding cry of an heroic people,
And the dazzling rays of the sun of Liberty
Bathed our country in their brilliant light.

If with strong arm we have succeeded
In winning a pledge of equality,
In thy bosom, O Liberty,
Our hearts will defy death itself!

O adored Fatherland,
Cherished and revered,
All hail! All hail!

Brazil, a dream sublime, vivid ray of love and hope to earth descends,
Where in your clear, pure, beauteous skies
The image of the Southern Cross shines forth.

O country vast by nature,
Fair and strong, brave and colossus,
Thy future mirrors this thy greatness.

*(continues)*

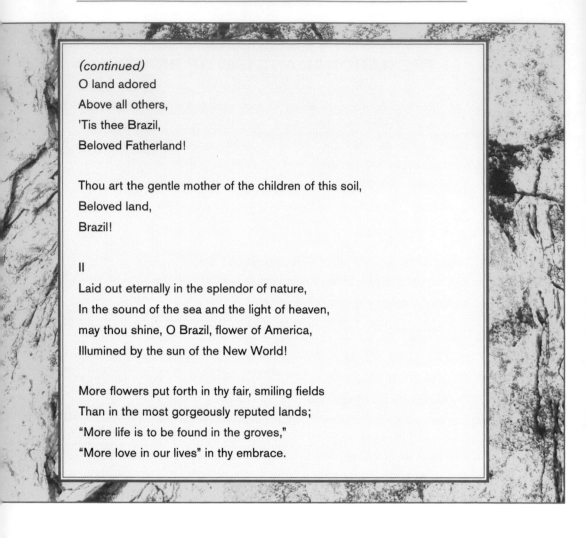

*(continued)*

O land adored
Above all others,
'Tis thee Brazil,
Beloved Fatherland!

Thou art the gentle mother of the children of this soil,
Beloved land,
Brazil!

II
Laid out eternally in the splendor of nature,
In the sound of the sea and the light of heaven,
may thou shine, O Brazil, flower of America,
Illumined by the sun of the New World!

More flowers put forth in thy fair, smiling fields
Than in the most gorgeously reputed lands;
"More life is to be found in the groves,"
"More love in our lives" in thy embrace.

with the ranchers. He granted their request and sent in approximately 50 police to protect the workers who were carrying out the clear-cutting.

Still, the rubber tappers refused to give up. They decided to stage a second *empate* despite the police presence. They recruited support from the Cachoeira estate, where more than 300 workers and their families had been camped out for weeks. Chico Mendes led more than 150 men, women, and children to the site that was

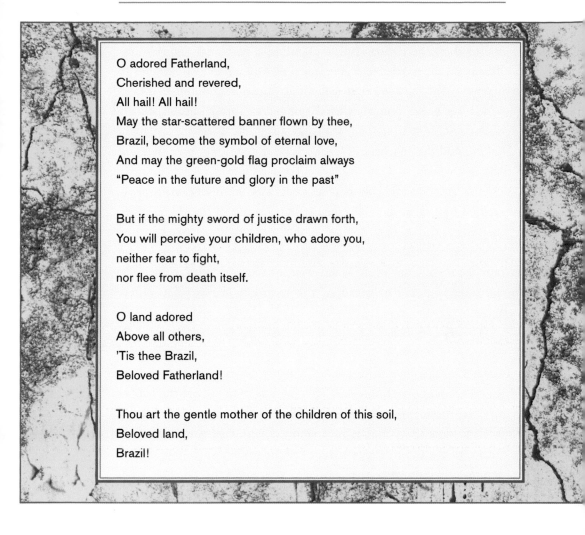

O adored Fatherland,
Cherished and revered,
All hail! All hail!
May the star-scattered banner flown by thee,
Brazil, become the symbol of eternal love,
And may the green-gold flag proclaim always
"Peace in the future and glory in the past"

But if the mighty sword of justice drawn forth,
You will perceive your children, who adore you,
neither fear to fight,
nor flee from death itself.

O land adored
Above all others,
'Tis thee Brazil,
Beloved Fatherland!

Thou art the gentle mother of the children of this soil,
Beloved land,
Brazil!

being cleared. School teachers and other members of the community came along with the rubber tappers.

As the group arrived at the site, the police moved in, ready to fire their weapons at the protestors. The women and children stood in front of the group, though, which prevented the police from opening fire.

Then, something amazing happened. Spontaneously, the school-teachers, women, and children began to sing the national anthem of Brazil. Soon, the entire group of rubber tappers were singing.

Because it was the national anthem, custom dictated that the police had to show their patriotism by standing at attention and saluting. "It was an indescribable scene," recalled Gomercindo Rodrigues in his book *Walking the Forest with Chico Mendes*. "I admit that even now I get goose bumps when I remember this scene, especially because it wasn't planned or discussed at the meeting the night before, and the teachers of Cachoeira did it on their own, without asking anybody."

The singing, and the moment of mutual patriotism it invoked, seemed to disarm the policemen in every sense of the word. When the song ended, Chico Mendes stepped forward and spoke with the commanding officer. He proposed that the police stop the deforestation just for one day while Mendes went to Xapuri to try to convince the forestry board to withdraw the clear-cut license. The officer agreed.

The forestry board refused to withdraw the license, but they did agree to have someone check on the deforestation operation and make sure the landowners weren't cutting down a bigger area than they were authorized to clear. This investigation proved the rubber tappers' suspicions to be correct. The landowners were preparing to clear more than double the amount of land that was authorized. Although the rubber tappers had been unsuccessful in stopping the deforestation altogether, at least they prevented the ranchers from clearing even more land than they were authorized to.

This was only a small victory. The rubber tappers wanted to stop all of the deforestation at the Ecuador estate, so they continued their fight. They staged another *empate* at the forestry board offices in Xapuri where they occupied the building. They demanded that the state government and the forestry board revoke Delta's license to clear the forest at Ecuador. One night, two men with guns drove by on a motorbike and shot at the protesters as they were sleeping on the porch, wounding two young rubber tappers. The motorbike was believed to belong to the son of Darli Alves da Silva, the owner of the Cachoeira estate against whom the rubber tappers had been battling for weeks.

The gunmen probably hoped that shooting the protestors would force them to back down and allow the deforestation to continue, but their plan had a fatal flaw. They hadn't taken into account that this time, Chico Mendes had international contacts and the attention of the media. People outside Brazil were already paying attention to the *empates,* and when the shootings occurred there was a huge outcry. The government in Acre was inundated with hundreds of telegrams from national and international environmental and human rights organizations pressuring the governor to withdraw the license. The media caught wind of the story and covered it extensively. Finally, the governor gave in to the pressure. The police were withdrawn, and Delta's license to clear the area was revoked. Although 123 acres (50 hectares) of forest were cleared before they were stopped, Mendes estimated that they had saved about 741 acres (300 hectares).

A second victory quickly followed, thanks to the pressure placed on the government after the shootings. In addition to stopping the clear-cutting at Ecuador, the government also took possession of the Cachoeira estate and allocated it to the rubber tappers. This was the first extractive reserve to be established in the Amazon rain forest.

After the Cachoeira estate had been allocated to the rubber tappers, two more reserves encompassing about 150 square miles (241 sq. km) each were declared in quick succession. The movement seemed to be gaining momentum. Mendes noted that the victory at Cachoeira, where close to 400 rubber tappers had participated, gave the movement a huge boost in morale and made the rubber tappers even more determined to keep fighting.

## RETALIATION

Although the movement to protect the rain forest was finally seeing some progress, the Cachoeira victory was also a dangerous turning point in the life of Chico Mendes. The rancher Darli Alves da Silva, who had lost his land to the rubber tappers, was angry. He decided that Mendes and the rubber tappers had to be stopped once and for all. Determined to exact revenge, he began making threats on Mendes's life.

This wasn't the first time Mendes's life had been threatened. He had been receiving death threats from ranchers since 1977. Mendes also had information that on the day Wilson Pinheiro was assassinated back in 1980, he had also been targeted to be killed. By sheer luck, the gunmen assigned to kill him never found him. Mendes was followed by gunmen for weeks following Pinheiro's death and had to go into hiding for about two months. Attempts on his life continued over the years, and to his knowledge, he had come close to being killed at least six times. Each time, he either managed to escape by chance, or had received warnings and changed his plans to escape the gunmen.

Throughout the last part of 1988, after Darli Alves da Silva lost his land to the rubber tappers, the ranchers called for an increase in violent retaliation against the rubber tappers who resisted them. Shortly after the shootings at the forestry board, another union organizer was killed. In general, violence in and around Xapuri intensified as the year went on, but the ranchers' ultimate target was Chico Mendes—and Mendes knew it.

In fact, Mendes had gathered evidence that Alves da Silva had plans to have him and other leaders of the rubber tapper movement killed. He tried to get law enforcement to follow through on this evidence, but it soon became clear that the legal system was going to provide more protection for the cattle ranchers than for Mendes. In July of 1988, Mendes uncovered an old judge's order to arrest and imprison Darli Alves da Silva and his brother Alvarino for a murder that had occurred in 1973—the year before the Alves da Silva family had moved to Xapuri. He showed this order to the police, but they still did not act on it. Mendes persisted in his efforts, though, and, in October, a judge from Xapuri ordered military police to arrest the two men. Unfortunately, they had gone into hiding. Mendes believed they had been tipped off by the police chief to whom Mendes had shown the arrest warrant in July. His efforts to expose the brothers for their past crimes only intensified their desire to silence him.

Mendes continued to write letters to the police, accusing them of protecting the Alves da Silva family and their hired gunmen. Throughout the year, he gathered evidence and tried to get the police to act. For the most part, these warnings went unheeded. The media and politicians in Acre dismissed his claims, saying he was only trying to get his name in the paper. The police force's refusal to act led some people to believe that the Alves da Silva plot to assassinate Mendes was more than a personal vendetta against Mendes for leading the Cachoeira *empate*. Many believed that it was part of a wider conspiracy on the part of the UDR and the government to derail the rubber-tapper movement altogether by silencing its leader.

As 1988 drew to a close, Mendes continued to travel around Brazil, giving speeches and spreading the word about what was happening in the rain forest. In December, he travelled to Sao Paulo and Rio de Janeiro, two cities in the southern part of Brazil. These wealthy, industrialized cities were worlds apart from the life Mendes led in the Amazon. While there, Mendes stayed in the comfortable, modern apartments of friends in the environmental movement. These homes were a stark contrast to the simple shacks and cottages Mendes had lived in all of his life in the rain forest.

Meanwhile, the threats against Mendes intensified and became more ominous. In early December, a local newspaper that was owned by a UDR leader published an ominous note that said simply: "Very soon a 200-megaton bomb will explode and the repercussions will be country-wide. Important people may get hurt by the end of the story. Wait and see because our source is trustworthy." Below this strange note was an article criticizing Chico Mendes.

By this time, Mendes had seemed to accept that his assassins would eventually catch up with him. His speeches took on the air of a final farewell. He started saying goodbye to his friends and supporters as if for the last time. He took every opportunity to warn people about his impending assassination in hopes that he would not die in vain. On December 6, 1988, in a speech at a university in Sao Paulo, he said, "I don't want flowers because I know you are going to pull them up from the forest. The only thing I want is that my death helps to stop the murderers' impunity. [They] are under the protection of the Acre police, and who, since 1975, have killed more than 50 people in the rural zone."

Throughout this time, Mendes reported being followed by gunmen and received multiple telephone threats at the union office. According to Andrew Revkin, author of the book *The Burning Season*, Mendes visited his brother, Zuza, who was a rubber tapper on the Santa Fe estate in mid-December and told him that he had received several phone calls telling him that he was going to die. "I have a feeling I'm not going to make it to Christmas," he predicted. His brother urged him to go into hiding until the threats subsided, but Mendes insisted on continuing his work. "I've been fighting here for more than 20 years, together with the comrades. I've never run away and I've never sold out. I'm not going to run away now," he told his brother.

A few days before Christmas, Mendes returned home to Xapuri to be with his wife and children. His friends urged him to stay away, fearing that Alves da Silva's hired gunmen would finally catch up to him in his hometown. Again, Mendes refused to run scared. He insisted on being with his family for Christmas. Many of his friends reported that he was resolved to meet his fate head on, whatever that might be.

By this time, he and Ilza had managed to acquire a house of their own with the financial help of several of Mendes's friends from the environmental movement. Their little blue and pink cottage had four rooms and was approximately the size of a one-car garage. Like the other homes on their street, the house was built on stilts to keep it off the moist rain forest ground. The only running water was located in an outdoor bathroom behind the cottage.

Mendes spent the next few days with his family. A new truck had recently been donated to the Xapuri Rural Workers' Union, and, on December 22, he took his young son and daughter out for a ride in the new truck, stopping often to catch up with friends in the area. Ilza recalled that Mendes was unusually attentive to his

Chico Mendes's home (*center*) in Xapuri is now a museum.

children that day. "He would stop to kiss them all the time," she told August Dwyer, author of *Into the Amazon: The Struggle for the Rain Forest*. During this drive around town, Mendes stopped at the local hospital to pick up medicine to distribute on the reserves. His sister also worked there, and, as he had with others, he confided to her that he did not expect to live much longer.

Was Chico Mendes afraid to die? By all accounts, no. As the year drew to the close, and the threats on his life became more ominous, Mendes seemed to accept that his assassination was inevitable. By December, each time he predicted his death, he seemed to be saying goodbye to his supporters, his friends, and his family. They all reported that he did so without any sign of fear or anxiety. When he saw his brother Zuza in mid-December, he told him that he dreamed that he saw their mother (who had died when he was a teenager) smiling and waving to him from a field of flowers where she had made a comfortable bed for him.

However, this acceptance does not mean that Mendes had given up, or that he wanted to die. He could have given in, or gone into hiding, or even left the country, but he remained committed to his movement until the end. While he wanted to escape the gunmen so he could continue his work, he also understood that, with the protection provided to the ranchers by the police and a sympathetic legal system, it was unlikely that he would manage to dodge them forever. According to his friends, he seemed to have made his peace with this inevitable fact. He seemed to take comfort in the idea that his movement would go on without him. "I don't get that cold feeling anymore. I am no longer afraid of dying and I know they can't destroy us," he said in *Fight for the Forest*. "If any of us got killed, the resistance would still go on and it might even be that much stronger."

Because Mendes had been so vocal about the threats on his life, the military police had finally agreed to assign two guards to protect him. They were young and inexperienced and had only one revolver between them. They stayed with Mendes until dark each day and became family friends.

On the night of December 22, 1988, Mendes sat in his kitchen playing dominoes, his favorite game, with his guards and his friend, Gomercindo Rodrigues. Ilza was getting ready to make dinner, and their two children, ages two and four, were watching television in the next room. Gomercindo left to run an errand, promising to return for dinner.

The night was hot and sticky, and Mendes got up to cool off in the backyard shower stall (there was no running water inside the house). When he realized the light bulb in the outhouse had burned out, he got a flashlight and opened the back door. Instead of following him, the two guards remained seated at the table.

Two gunmen, hired by the Alves da Silvas, had been hiding patiently in the bushes behind the Mendes's house for several days, armed with shotguns and waiting for their chance. They were so quiet that not even the many neighborhood dogs and chickens were alert to their presence. When Mendes opened the back door to head to the outhouse, they didn't hesitate. They shot Mendes squarely in the chest. Mendes stumbled back into the house. No one, not even the guards, dared to open the door again and go after the gunmen. Mendes died moments later.

## AFTERMATH

After Mendes collapsed, the two guards fled the little house through a window that opened onto the street—not to chase down the gunmen, but to return to the safety of the police barracks. Ilza ran out into the street and shouted, "They've killed Chico!" Many of their neighbors had heard the shots. Guessing what must have happened, they were already running over to the Mendes household to see if they could help. Meanwhile, the policemen who were sitting outside the barracks just down the street did nothing in response to Ilza's cries. No one chased after the gunmen.

News of Mendes's death spread quickly. A municipal radio station where Darli Alves da Silva's half-brother worked reported the news within 15 minutes of the shooting. Journalists from other parts of Brazil appeared in Xapuri within an hour, and, the next day, the story was on the front page of many Brazilian newspapers.

The news of Mendes's murder did not stop at the borders of Brazil. If the people who had planned Mendes's murder had hoped that his death would be seen as just another incident of rural violence in the Amazon, they were wrong. Once again, they had miscalculated the level of support and attention Mendes had among environmentalists outside Brazil. It took mere hours for the international media to report Mendes's death, and an international outcry ensued. The Brazilian government would not be allowed to sweep Mendes's death under the rug: The world was watching, and the police were now under great pressure to catch those responsible.

Luiz Inácio da Silva, who later became the president of Brazil (2003–2011), delivers a speech at Chico Mendes's funeral in Rio Branco, Acre, on December 25, 1988.

Raimundo Mendes de Barros, Chico Mendes's cousin, stands in the doorway of the rubber tappers' union in November 1989. The banner hanging outside says *Basta!*, meaning "Enough!", referring to the violent turn in the struggle to protect the Amazon.

Chico Mendes's funeral was held at a cathedral in Xapuri on Christmas Day. It was attended by about 2,000 mourners from all over Brazil. Hundreds of rubber tappers traveled for miles by foot to say goodbye to their beloved leader. Environmentalists, politicians, union leaders, and celebrities from all over Brazil also came. The simple Catholic ceremony was followed by several speeches from union leaders, who demanded justice for Mendes's death and vowed to continue his work. According to a December 26, 1988 *Washington Post* article, the head of Brasiléia's rural workers' union declared, "Not one more tree will be cut down in Acre."

In January, another memorial service was held for Mendes in Washington, D.C. More than 300 environmentalists, political activists, politicians, religious leaders, journalists, and friends came together to grieve Mendes's untimely death. His cousin Raimundo Barros was flown in from Brazil to give the eulogy. Mendes was remembered by these mourners primarily as an ecologist who gave his life to save the rain forest.

## UNANSWERED QUESTIONS

Although it was satisfying for Mendes's supporters to see two of his killers go to prison, many believed that Darci Alves Pereira and Darli Alves da Silva were not the true masterminds of the plot to assassinate Mendes. It was true that Darli had several personal reasons for killing Mendes, mainly to get revenge for losing his investment in the Cachoeira estate. Still, it was widely believed that the murder was actually orchestrated by a wider conspiracy of powerful landowners, law enforcement officials, and politicians who were becoming more and more worried about Mendes's rising popularity and the momentum of his movement. Some believe that these forces simply took advantage of Darli Alves da Silva's desire for revenge and his violent tendencies to get him to do the dirty work for them.

One piece of evidence that the murder was part of a deeper conspiracy is the ominous note that was run a few days before Mendes's death in the UDR-backed paper *O Rio Branco*, discussed earlier. The note indicates that staff at the newspaper knew about the plot to kill Mendes in advance.

In addition, many people were suspicious about the inexplicably fast arrival of a news team from *O Rio Branco* after Mendes's death. Reporters arrived on the scene in Xapuri just 90 minutes after the shooting. According to Tony Gross, in *Fight for the Forest*, the

## INVESTIGATION, ARREST, AND TRIAL

On December 23, 1988, a special police inspector was assigned to investigate the case. Forensic evidence at the gunmen's hideout behind the Mendes's house indicated that Darli Alves da Silva's son, Darci, had been at the scene and perhaps even fired the fatal shot. An additional gunman, a ranch hand of the Alves da Silvas, was also identified.

journey takes at least three hours in good weather. For the news team to make it to Xapuri in less than two hours at night during the rainy season was virtually impossible. Furthermore, military policemen noted that the engine of the truck that the reporters arrived in wasn't even hot when they arrived. The next day, the paper ran a front-page story on the murder. Many believed it was obvious that the journalists knew beforehand that Mendes would be killed that night and were already in Xapuri, waiting.

On December 17, a doctor with a practice in Acre was playing cards in a club in Rio Branco. One of the men at his table began bragging that Chico Mendes would be dead within five days. He claimed that a truck was waiting outside ready to take weapons to Xapuri. That truck belonged to the mayor of Rio Branco, and was driven by one of the mayor's bodyguards. The doctor tried to alert the police, but, again, these warnings were ignored. The apparent involvement of the mayor of Rio Branco indicates that this plot went beyond the lawless UDR movement and may very well have involved politicians and members of local government.

Was the murder of Chico Mendes simply an act of revenge, or was it a wider conspiracy, an attempt to squash the rubber tappers' movement to stop deforestation? This is a question that may never be answered with certainty. The Brazilian police force's investigations never looked beyond the Alves da Silva family.

Ilza Mendes sits in the back of a truck with other activists on the way to Rio Branco to demonstrate and attend a tribunal hearing regarding the possibility of a trial for her husband's suspected killers.

The police began searching for Darci and Darli as well as Darli's brother, Alvarino, and the hired gunman. Eventually, Darci and Darli both turned themselves in to the police. The father and son were held for trial. However, Alvarino and the second gunman were never caught. In 1990, Darli and Darci were convicted of premeditated murder and sentenced to 19 years in prison. They both escaped in 1993, but Darli was recaptured and returned to prison to serve out his sentence.

# The Legacy of
# Chico Mendes

Before his death, Chico Mendes had become well known outside Brazil for his work leading the rubber tappers' movement. After he was killed, he and his cause became even more famous both within Brazil and around the world. The situation in the Amazon, including deforestation and the violence and general lawlessness that existed there, was revealed to the world. The Brazilian government faced increased pressure from environmental organizations, human-rights groups, the media, governments, and politicians to change their policy regarding the Amazon.

## POLICY CHANGES IN BRAZIL

In early 1989, Brazilian president José Sarney took steps to completely reorganize the federal agencies related to forestry and the environment. He combined them into one federal institute called the Brazilian Institute for the Environment and Renewable Natural Resources (IBAMA), indicating a shift in priorities from developing the Amazon to conserving its natural resources. The government also announced a new environmental initiative called Our Nature, but this was widely viewed as inadequate because it was primarily aimed at improving Brazil's image rather than improving its actual environmental policy.

The effectiveness of IBAMA was in doubt, as well. The primary goal of the agency was to create a forest protection service. However, the agency did not have enough funding to do this adequately. The first president of IBAMA was a man named Fernando César Mesquita. He left the position in March 1990, complaining that IBAMA did not have the means to follow through on its promises. The agency was understaffed and didn't even have helicopters to monitor the forest during the burning season of 1989.

Perhaps the most effective step Sarney took to protect the forest was to suspend the tax incentives given to ranchers that had been initiated by the military government back in the 1960s to encourage development of the Amazon. Without these incentives, land speculators and ranchers had less motivation to buy up land and clear the forest.

## THE CHICO MENDES EXTRACTIVE RESERVE

Despite Mesquita's frustrations with IBAMA, he did achieve one very important thing for the rubber tappers. In January 1990, he persuaded President Sarney to issue a decree that established the extractive-reserve concept in the way that Chico Mendes had always envisioned. This decree allowed the state to take possession of blocks of land and work with the local community to develop a plan for how the forest dwellers could use the land for economic gain without damaging the forest. There would be no private property on the reserves, and no outsiders would be permitted to acquire land there.

Immediately upon establishing the extractive-reserve concept, President Sarney signed another decree creating the first real extractive reserve, which covered 1,235,526 acres (500,000 hectares) of rain forest land in western Acre. In March, he also established a huge, 2,471,053-acre (one-million-hectare) reserve stretching across Brasiléia, Xapuri, and Rio Branco. It was named the Chico Mendes Extractive Reserve. Extractive reserves were also created in the states of Amapá and Rondonia.

Unfortunately, IBAMA continued to have problems getting enough funding. In March 1990, President Sarney left office and was replaced by President Collor. Collor's economic policies limited the funds available to IBAMA even more. This made it difficult for the agency to be effective in its efforts to protect conservation lands, including the extractive reserves.

Even so, deforestation declined between 1989 and 1991. Between 1978 and 1988, annual forest loss was approximately 13,000 square miles (21,000 sq. km). In 1989, it was estimated to be about 11,000 square miles (17,800 sq. km) and in 1991, the number went down to about 6,800 square miles (11,000 sq. km). The combination of national policy change, the extractive reserves, and the removal of tax incentives for clearing the forest seemed to be having an effect.

## THE FIGHT FOR LAND CONTINUES

Although the extractive reserves instated by President Sarney were a positive step, the rubber tappers of the Amazon still had many fights ahead of them to preserve their way of life in the forest. President Sarney and President Collor both took positive steps but did not

(opposite page) The fight to save the rain forest brought people with like minds together, and Chico Mendes aided by creating an alliance between the rubber tappers and the Indians, called Peoples of the Forest Alliance. Pictured at their second meeting in March 1989, after Mendes's death, are an Ashaninka Indian (*left*) and Julio Barbosa (*right*), who was a friend of Mendes and later Xapuri's mayor.

follow through with adequate funding for enforcing their policies. In addition, the powerful ranchers and landowners were still determined to maintain their hold on rain-forest land and expand their ranching and agricultural operations.

In November 1990, local elections were held and brought in a new crop of leaders who were mostly sympathetic with the ranchers and unfriendly to the rubber tappers' cause. Some measures that had been taken to regulate deforestation were dismantled. For example, since 1988, ranchers in Acre had been required to provide environmental-impact reports and appear at a public hearing before getting permission to clear the forest. However, the new administration in Acre repealed this policy.

With the local government still friendly toward the ranchers and other developers, these powerful landowners continued to acquire land and clear the forest—often illegally. Rubber tappers were still losing their homesteads and the ancient forest continued to burn. The leaders of the Rural Workers' Unions and the CNS continued to organize and fight for the rubber tappers and organize *empates*. The national policy shift had helped preserved some of the forest, but the lack of enforcement made it seem as if little had changed on the local level. In his book *Fight for the Forest*, Tony Gross posited that rubber tappers and other rural workers were actually worse off by the early 1990s than they had been before Mendes's death.

The landowners continued to use brutal and violent means to maintain their hold on forest land. The leaders of the rural workers' unions and the CNS continued to live in fear of assassination. According to Tony Gross, the presidents of the Rural Workers' Union in Brasiléia and the CNS, as well as other prominent activists, received multiple death threats after Mendes was killed. In 1991, Pedro Ramos de Souza, the vice president of the CNS, protested the building of a government road through an extractive reserve and was subsequently attacked and beaten in retaliation. Many other leaders were threatened and attacked.

Sadly, violence and lawlessness are still the norm in the Amazon, where the fight over land continues to this day. According to a

# DOROTHY STANG: 1931–2005

In 2005, the world was reminded of the violent battles over land that still prevail in the Amazon today when Sister Dorothy Stang, an American nun, was assassinated in the Amazon.

Dorothy Stang was born in Dayton, Ohio, in 1931. She was in high school when she decided to become a nun. She joined the Sisters of Notre Dame de Namure in Cincinnati, Ohio—an order which focuses on social justice and taking "our stand with poor people, especially women and

U.S. missionary Dorothy Stang, shown here in 2004, attracted criticism from local farmers for trying to implement an unprecedented sustainability project within a large section of the Amazon.

children, in the most abandoned places." Sister Stang dedicated her life to these beliefs.

In the 1960s, she arrived in the state of Pará, Brazil. She settled in the town of Anapu, on the edge of the rain forest, and dedicated the rest of her life to protecting the rain forest and its people from loggers and ranchers. There she became known among the local peasants as "the angel of the Trans-Amazonian."

In Pará, there were many poor families who had come to the region as a result of the 1960s government program to encourage settlement of the Amazon. Sister Stang worked to improve the lives of the

*(continues)*

*(continued)*

poor farmers in the region: She helped them start small businesses, built schools, trained teachers, and worked to improve healthcare.

At the same time, she also worked to protect the peasants from the powerful landowners—loggers and ranchers—who began arriving in the region and illegally pushing the peasants off their land and taking possession of it. Like Chico Mendes, she dreamed of the region becoming a haven of sustainable development projects, where poor farmers could live in harmony with the forest.

Although she was viewed as a hero among the peasants, loggers viewed her as a terrorist, and she soon joined other activists on a list of people marked to be assassinated. Sister Stang told concerned friends that her status as a nun and her age would protect her from being assassinated. She was wrong. On February 12, 2005, as she was walking with two peasants to a meeting about 30 miles (48 km) from her home, she was shot and killed by two gunmen.

She was the most prominent rain-forest activist to be killed since Chico Mendes. Again, her death resulted in an international outcry and increased awareness of the complex problems in the Amazon. Thousands attended her funeral in Pará, and memorial services were held for her around the world. Following her death, the Brazilian government recommitted itself to creating more reserves and putting a stop to illegal deforestation. Two thousand military troops were sent to the area to stop the violence.

The Brazilian police and the U.S. Federal Bureau of Investigation both investigated Stang's murder, determined to find and jail the masterminds and not just the gunmen they hired to assassinate the nun. In spring of 2010, ranchers Regivaldo Galvao and Vitalmiro Bastos de Moura were convicted of ordering Stang's murder and sentenced to 30 years in jail.

December 21, 2008, article on msnbc.com, more than 1,100 activists, rural workers, priests, and judges were killed between Mendes's 1988 death and 2008. Fewer than 100 of those murders were ever brought to court. According to the Catholic Land Pastoral, about 80 of the killers were hired by ranchers and loggers to silence people who stood in the way of their efforts to increase their landholdings. Of the people behind the killings, 15 of them have been tried in court and found guilty, but only a few of them served time in jail for their crimes.

## ENVIRONMENTAL AND ECONOMIC POLICIES AT ODDS

Although there was a sharp decline in forest loss in the first years after Chico Mendes's death, the number of acres lost per year soon began to climb again. According to Dr. Stephen Schwartzman of the Environmental Defense Fund, in his 1999 article, "Ten Years After the Death of Chico Mendes: The Amazon in the New Millennium," from 1989 to 1999 the rain forest was burned at a rate of at least 13,000 acres per day (5,260 hectares)—or 8 football fields per minute. Schwartzman notes that these are Brazil's official estimates, and some researchers believe that the numbers may be significantly higher.

Part of the problem for Brazil is that its economic and environmental policies are at odds with one another. Following the international outcry after Chico Mendes's murder, the country's leadership has pledged to do a better job of protecting the rain forest and its people. On the other hand, Brazil has a crippling national debt and, as a result, the World Bank has pressured the country to develop the Amazon economically in order to generate income to repay this debt. This pressure is primarily what has driven the expansion of logging, cattle ranching, and other development in the rain-forest region.

Several industries are now contributing to the rapid destruction of the rain forest. Although cattle ranching was the primary threat in Acre during Chico Mendes's time, in other Amazonian states, such as Pará, commercial logging was a dominant force in forest destruction. The wood from many types of tropical trees—such as teak, mahogany, and rosewood—is exported to developed countries and used to make furniture, building materials, and even charcoal. Even more wood is harvested from the rain forest to make cardboard and paper products.

Soya farming is another large-scale agriculture venture that is contributing to the destruction of the Amazon. Soybeans are processed and used to feed the cattle raised in the Amazon. In addition, the beans are exported and processed for use in a wide variety of

More than a thousand people march in the city of Santarem in Pará to ask for protection of the Amazon rain forest from rampant destruction caused by soya expansion. The march ended in front of a Cargill factory.

food products, including animal feed, soybean oil, infant formula, and as a filler in many prepackaged meats. Soya is cultivated on a large scale in the Amazon by large multinational corporations, such as Cargill, the Minnesota-based food conglomerate. Some believe that if Cargill had not installed a soybean washer and dryer in the Amazon, there would have been little incentive to cultivate the plant there, since the beans will spoil if not cleaned and dried before being transported out of the Amazon.

## SIGNS OF HOPE

In recent years, there has been some progress in the fight to save the rain forest. Much of this has been the result of pressure from environmental activists on the Brazilian government as well as the large corporations who are driving much of the deforestation.

For example, in 2006, Greenpeace United Kingdom (UK) ran a campaign accusing large beef distributors in Europe, including fast-food chains and supermarkets, of indirectly driving the destruction of the rain forest for soybean farming. Greenpeace UK argued that by purchasing massive amounts of beef raised in the Amazon for sale in restaurants throughout Europe, these corporations were helping to encourage the destruction of the forest for large-scale agricultural operations—and the violence and land-grabbing that comes with it.

As a result of the Greenpeace campaign, several of the corporations targeted worked with Greenpeace UK to develop a "zero deforestation plan." They now use their significant buying power to demand that the soy and soy-fed meat products they purchase are not cultivated on newly cleared rain-forest land. In turn, this put pressure on the large corporations behind soybean farming to commit to a two-year moratorium on buying soybeans from deforested areas. In 2009, Greenpeace UK also convinced four of the largest cattle companies in the world to agree to a similar moratorium on purchasing beef raised on deforested land.

*(continues on page 106)*

# ELENIRA MENDES:
# THE VANGUARD OF HOPE

Elenira Mendes was just four years old when her father was murdered right before her eyes. What she didn't know then was that her father had already named her to carry on his movement after he died. In 2005, when Elenira was 20 years old, she discovered a note her father had written to her before his death. Attached to the note was a picture of Elenira as a child. The note read:

"You are the vanguard of hope, Elenira—one day you will continue the fight that your father will not be able to win."

Perhaps it is fitting that Elenira first found this note when she was 20 years old—old enough to begin to take on the work her father left for her. In 2006, she founded the Chico Mendes Institute in Xapuri, Mendes's hometown. As chairperson of the Chico Mendes Institute, Elenira works to carry on her father's legacy of protecting both the rubber tappers and the rain forest on which they depend.

Despite the cynicism and disappointment that many Chico Mendes supporters feel in regard to what they see as weak changes in Brazil's policy regarding the Amazon, Elenira believes that significant progress has been made in establishing sustainable development practices throughout the Amazon since her father's death. However, there is still work to be done to achieve her father's vision for the rain forest and its people. She insists on carrying on her father's idealism and sees those ideals as being "very much alive among our people, the people of my father's and my state, Acre."

On the twentieth anniversary of her father's death, Elenira posted this letter to Chico Mendes on a friend's blog:

"Unfortunately, we are still only dreaming in search of a better society. It has been 20 years since that night, when I saw you for the last time . . . trying to tell us, me and my mother, something we never knew exactly what. Father, be sure that your fight was not in vain. Your dreams are no longer only yours. They are also mine and of all those who still believe in your ideals.

You are still the vanguard of hope for the Amazon and our beloved Acre."

Fifteen years after Chico Mendes's death, his children Elenira and Sandino pose in the home in which they once lived. Elenira, who has a degree in business and is now studying law, directs the Chico Mendes Foundation. Sandino also continues his father's legacy by working with the rubber tappers.

*(continued from page 103)*

## A NEW EQUATION: MAKING SAVING THE RAIN FOREST PROFITABLE

As you have read, the destruction of the rain forest is being driven by economics. The Brazilian government needs to generate income to offset its national debt. Brazilian land speculators, ranchers, and multinational corporations seek to profit from this by buying up inexpensive land in the rain forest and clearing it for timber and agricultural use. Yet, these profits are primarily short-term, especially as more and more cleared rain-forest land becomes unusable.

Chico Mendes knew that the only way to save the rain forest was to offer ways to profit from its resources without destroying it. This is a fundamental truth that still applies today. According to Rain-tree.com, a landowner profits about $60 per acre raising cattle on cleared rain-forest land and about $400 per acre from logging. Yet, if medicinal plants, fruits, nuts, rubber, and other renewable resources were harvested, a landowner could profit $2,400 from an acre of intact rain forest land.

To this end, some rain-forest activists are looking to pharmaceutical companies to help drive a new, sustainable rain forest economy. Currently, more than 100 drug companies, as well as the U.S. government, are conducting research on the medicinal potential of plants in the rain forest. This new field is called bioprospecting. Researchers are working with indigenous groups who understand the medicinal properties of many rain-forest plants. If researchers can prove that the rain forest is far more valuable economically if left intact, there would be more motivation on the part of governments and citizens to put a stop to deforestation for short-term economic gain.

These are all positive signs that the economic motivation for deforestation may one day see its end. But in the meantime, Chico Mendes's beloved forest is still burning. The powerful landowners who had Chico Mendes and Dorothy Stang killed are still entrenched in the forest. Many rubber tappers are still fighting to hold onto their livelihood. The vast, ancient rain forest, and all it means for life on Earth, is still threatened.

Brazil's first female president, Dilma Rousseff (*left*), sits next to Chico Mendes's oldest child, Angela, at a pre-election Worker's Party Rally geared toward the subject of the environment in October 2010.

In the Amazon, many brave people have carried on Mendes's work in hopes that he did not die in vain. Yet time and again, it has been proven that they can only accomplish so much on their own to fight the corruption, power, and greed that have driven the destruction of the rain forest. It is a combination of the activists within the country and the continued international pressure on the Brazilian government and the corporations that is helping to turn the tide. This collection of voices—the rubber tappers, the Indians, environmentalists, politicians, and corporations—must be loud enough to drown out the sound of chainsaws and destruction.

In 1999, Dr. Stephen Schwartzman of the U.S.-based Environmental Defense Fund explained in an article, "Chico Mendes, rubber tapper, union leader, environmentalist, and citizen, was a butterfly flapping his wings over the forest. He started a storm that is still rising over the Amazon and may yet reach around the world in unpredictable ways."

# How to Get Involved

These organizations provide information and other resources related to rain forests and conservation.

**Environmental Defense Fund**
257 Park Avenue South
New York, NY 10010
(212) 505–2100
*www.edf.org*
The Environmental Defense Fund (EDF) uses a variety of strategies to tackle the world's environmental threats. Dr. Stephen Schwartzman, an anthropologist for the EDF, worked closely with Chico Mendes in the 1970s and 1980s.

**Greenpeace**
702 H Street, NW, Suite 300
Washington, D.C. 2000
(202) 462–1177
*www.greenpeace.org*
Greenpeace uses nonviolent means to expose and find solutions to environmental problems such as the destruction of ancient forests and climate change.

**Kids Saving the Rainforest**
P.O. Box 297–6350
Quepos, Costa Rica 6350
*www.kidssavingtherainforest.org*
Kids Saving the Rainforest was founded in 1999 by two nine-year-old girls living in Costa Rica. Through a variety of projects, Kids Saving the Rainforest works to educate young people, preserve local rain-forest land, rescue and rehabilitate injured animals, and more.

**Rainforest Action Network**
221 Pine Street, 5th Floor
San Francisco, CA 94104
(415) 398-4404
*http://ran.org*
The Rainforest Action Network was founded in 1985 to protect the rain forest and the human rights of people living in and around the forest.

**The Rainforest Alliance**
665 Broadway, Suite 500
New York, NY 10012
(212) 677-1900
*www.rainforest-alliance.org*
The Rainforest Alliance works to promote sustainable land-use practice to conserve the forest and the livelihoods of the people who depend on it.

# Chronology

| | |
|---|---|
| **1944** | Chico Mendes is born in Xapuri, Acre. |
| **1962** | Mendes meets Euclides Távora who teaches him to read and encourages him to become politically active. |
| **1968** | Mendes marries Maria Eunice Feitosa; they have two daughters, Angela and Roseangela (the latter dies at 11 months old). |
| **1975** | Mendes joins the Rural Workers' Union in Brasiléia and is elected secretary. |
| **1977** | Mendes is elected to the municipal council in Xapuri. |
| **1978** | Mendes helps establish the union in Xapuri. |
| **1980** | The first *empates* are staged by the rubber tappers; Wilson Pinheiro is assassinated. |
| **1983** | Mendes and Ilzamar G. Bezerra are married. |
| **1984** | Mendes's daughter, Elenira, is born. |
| **1985** | First national Rubber Tappers' Congress is held in Brasièia, and the National Council of Rubber Tappers is founded. |
| **1986** | Mendes runs for the Acre state assembly, but is unsuccessful; Mendes's son, Sandino, is born. |
| **1987** | Mendes attends the governor's meeting of the Inter-American Development Bank and visits the United Kingdom; Mendes receives the "Global 500" award by the United Nations Environment Programme (UNEP). |
| **1988** | Mendes leads the Xapuri Rural Workers' Union in a successful attempt to stop cattle rancher Darli Alves da Silva from deforesting an area to be designated as an extractive reserve. |

**1988**        Mendes is assassinated outside his home by cattle
                ranchers Darli Alves da Silva and Darci Alves Pereira.

**1989**        President Sarney signs decrees creating the first
                extractive reserves in the Amazon, including the
                Chico Mendes Extractive Reserve in Acre.

**1990**        Darli Alves da Silva and Darci Alves Pereira are
                convicted of murder and sentenced to 19 years in
                prison.

# Glossary

**carbon emissions**  Carbon substances that are released into the atmosphere; most scientists believe carbon emissions are causing climate change.

**carbon sink**  A natural carbon storage system thought to help offset carbon emissions' effect on the global climate; the Amazon rain forest is one of the world's largest carbon sinks.

**coup d'etat**  The overthrow of an existing government by force

**crude**  Existing in a natural state, unaltered by cooking or processing

**dictatorship**  An authoritarian or totalitarian government, which gives absolute power to a single leader; it is the opposite of a democracy.

**ecosystem**  A system formed by the complex relationships between living organisms, resources, and their habitat in a specific area

**empate**  Term used to describe the rubber tappers' method of resisting deforestation by staging stand-offs with ranch workers

**exploitation**  The act of taking advantage of someone or something in an abusive or unfair manner

**extractive reserves**  Areas of publicly owned rain-forest land where rubber tappers and others have the right to live and harvest rubber, nuts, and other forest resources, without harming the forest

**idealism**  Having romantically optimistic beliefs about what is possible; Chico Mendes was idealistic because he never gave up on his hopes for saving the rain forest.

**indigenous**  Native; in this case, referring to the Indian groups that are native to the Amazon region

**latex**  A milky fluid produced by the cells of some seed plants; it is the source of rubber.

*seringals*  Rubber estates

*seringueiros*  Rubber tappers

**slash and burn**  Method of clearing the forest by which the vegetation is first chopped down and then burned to the ground

**trade union**  An organization made up of workers in a specific field that works to ensure fair treatment of its members by employers

# Bibliography

"About the Global 500." Global 500 Forum. Available online. http://www .global500.org/about.html. Accessed June 7, 2010.

"The Amazing Grace of Sister Dorothy Stang." The Sisters of Notre Dame de Namure. Available online. http://web.sndden.org/where/latin/brazil/ stang/index.htm. Accessed June 18, 2010.

"The Amazon Rainforest." BBC Online. February 14, 2003. Available online. http://www.bbc.co.uk/dna/h2g2/A925913. Accessed May 29, 2010.

"Analysis: Brazil Beef Industry Yields to Amazon Criticism." Reuters .com. June 29, 2009. Available online. http://www.reuters.com/assets/ print?aid=USN29452445. Accessed May 12, 2010.

The Chico Mendes Institute. http://www.chicomendes.org.br/index_ english.html. Accessed June 17, 2010.

Associated Press. "Amazon Killings Go on Despite Mendes' Legacy." December 21, 2008. Available online. MSNBC. http://www.msnbc .msn.com/id/28337919/. Accessed June 17, 2010.

Batty, David. "Brazilian Faces Retrial over Murder of Environmental Activist Nun in Amazon." *The Guardian*. April 8, 2009. Available online. http://www.guardian.co.uk/world/2009/apr/08/brazilian-murder-dorothy-stang. Accessed June 17, 2010.

"Brazil Generals' Coup (1964)." Global Security. 2009. Available online. http://www.globalsecurity.org/military/world/war/brazil.htm. Accessed March 1, 2010.

Buncombe, Andrew. "The Life and Brutal Death of Sister Dorothy, a Rainforest Martyr." February 15, 2005. *The Independent*. Available online. http://www.commondreams.org/headlines05/1215–03.htm. Accessed June 17, 2010.

Butler, Rhett. "Cattle Pastures." 2010. Mongabay.com. http://rainforests .mongabay.com/0812.htm. Accessed June 16, 2010.

———"Deforestation in the Amazon." Mongabay.com. Available online. http://www.mongabay.com/brazil.html. Accessed June 10, 2010.

**114**

Cappato, Jorge. "Who Was Chico Mendes?" UNEP Global 500 Forum. Available online. http://www.global500.org/feature_6.html. Accessed February 6, 2010.

"The Chico Mendes Story." WorldWrite: Brazil Exchange. (No Date). Available online. http://worldwrite.org.uk/site/brazil/mendes.html. Accessed March 31, 2010.

Connor, Steve. "Revenge of the Rain Forest." *The Independent.* March 6, 2009. Available online. http://www.independent.co.uk/environment/climate-change/revenge-of-the-rainforest-1638524.html. Accessed May 14, 2010.

de Deus Matos Gatatildeo, Atanagildo. "The Ideas of Chico Mendes and the National Council of Rubber Tappers." Environmental Defense Fund. May 29, 2009. Available online. http://www.edf.org/article.cfm?ContentID=1552. Accessed February 9, 2010.

"The 'Development' of the Amazon—Cattle Raising." Amazonlink.org. Available online. http://www.amazonlink.org/ACRE/amazonas/rubber-tappers/cattle.htm. Accessed June 16, 2010.

Dorothy Stang. Available online. http://dorothystang.org. Accessed June 17, 2010.

Dwyer, Augusta. *Into the Amazon: The Struggle for the Rainforest.* Toronto: Seal Books. 1990.

"Environmental Defense Fund and Chico Mendes: A Brief History of Their Work Together." June 1, 1999. Environmental Defense Fund. Available online. http://www.edf.org/article.cfm?ContentID=1600. Accessed June 7, 2010.

"Evaluate: The Slash and Burn Threat." Thinkquest. 1999. Available online. http://library.thinkquest.org/26252/evaluate/11.htm. Accessed May 12, 2010.

"Events in the Life of Chico Mendes." Environmental Defense Fund. May 27, 2009. Available online. http://www.edf.org/article.cfm?ContentID=1605. Accessed March 31, 2010.

"Extreme Drought in the Amazon Rain Forest Linked to Deforestation and Climate Change." Greenpeace. October 18, 2005. Available online. http://www.greenpeace.org/international/en/press/releases/ extreme-drought-in-the-amazon/. Accessed May 14, 2010.

Field Sites. Amazon Conservation Association. Available online. http://www.amazonconservation.org/about/fieldsites.html. Accessed March 1, 2010.

Gore, Al. *An Inconvenient Truth*. Emmaus, Penn.: Rodale, 2006.

Hey, Andrew. "U.S. Nun, Amazon Forest Activist, Murdered in Brazil." February 13, 2005. Reuters. Available online. http://www.common dreams.org/headlines/05/0213–05.htm. Accessed June 17, 2010.

"How Cattle Ranches Are Chewing Up the Forest." January 2009. Greenpeace UK. Available online. http://www.greenpeace.org.uk/blog/ forests/how-cattle-ranching-chewing-amazon-rainforest-20090129. Accessed June 6, 2010.

Hudson, Rex A., ed. *Brazil: A Country Study*. Washington: GPO for the Library of Congress, 1997. Available online. http://countrystudies/us/ brazil. Accessed June 15, 2010.

Ireland, Timothy. "Literacy in Brazil." National Research and Development Centre for Adult Literacy and Numeracy. (No date). Available online. http://www.nrdc.org.uk/content.asp?CategoryID=1033. June 6, 2010.

"Jaguar." National Geographic Online. 2009. Available online. http:// animals.nationalgeographic.com/animals/printalbe/jaguar. Accessed April 20, 2010.

"Jaguar (Panther Onca)." Rainforest Alliance. 2010. Available online. http:// www.rainforest-alliance.org/resources.cfm?id=jaguar. Accessed April 20, 2010.

Literate Brazil Programme. UNESCO. 2009. Available online. http://www .unesco.org/uil/litbase?menu=4&programme=50. Accessed June 6, 2010.

"Mary Allegretti." 2004 Annual Meeting Speaker Bios A-I. Philanthropy Roundtable. (2004). Available online. http://www.philanthropyround table.org/content.asp?contentid=505. Accessed June 8, 2010.

Mendes, Chico with Tony Gross. *Fight for the Forest: Chico Mendes in His Own Words*. London: Latin American Bureau, 1989.

Mendes, Elenira. "My Father's Legacy." Arts & Ecology. January 2009. Available online. http://www.chicomendes.org.br/index_english.html. Accessed June 17, 2010.

Monbiot, George. "The Price of Cheap Beef: Disease, Deforestation, Slavery and Murder." *The Guardian*. October 18, 2005. Available online. http://www.guardian.co.uk/uk/2005/oct/18/bse.foodanddrink. Accessed May 14, 2010.

Mori, Scott. "The Brazil Nut Industry—Past, Present and Future." In *Sustainable Harvest and Marketing of Rain Forest Products*. Washington, D.C.: Island Press, 1992.

The National Anthem of Brazil. Nederlanders in Brazil. Available online. http://www.wazamar.org/Nederlanders-in-Brazilie/a-volkslied-brazilie-tekst.htm. June 6, 2010.

Nix, Steve. "Tropical Rainforests and Biodiversity." About.com Forestry. 2010. Available online. http://forestry.about.com/cs/rainforest/p/rforest_diversi.htm?p=1. Accessed March 1, 2010.

"Rain Forest Facts: The Disappearing Rain Forests." 1986. Raintree Nutrition. Available online. http://www.rain-tree.com/facts.html. Accessed April 21, 2010.

Revkin, Andrew. *The Burning Season: The Murder of Chico Mendes*. Washington, D.C: Island Press, 2004.

Rodrigues, Gomercindo. *Walking the Forest with Chico Mendes*. Austin: University of Texas Press, 2007.

Schwartzman, Stephen. "Ten Years After the Death of Chico Mendes: The Amazon in the New Millenium." Environmental Defense Fund. June 1, 1999. Available online. http://edf.org/article.cfm?ContentID=1549. Accessed June 6, 2010.

"Thousands in Brazil Attend Slain Ecologist's Funeral." December 26, 1988. *The Washington Post*.

"Timeline: Brazil." BBC News. Available online. http://newsvote.bbc.co.uk.mpapps/pagetools/print/news.bbc.com. Accessed March 1, 2010.

Trussell, Jeff. "Earthkeeper Hero: Chico Mendes." The My Hero Project. Available online. http://www.myhero.com/go/print.asp?hero=c_mendes. February 9, 2010.

# Further Resources

## BOOKS

Goulding, Michael, Ronaldo Barthem, and Efrem Jorge Gondim Ferreira. *Smithsonian Atlas of the Amazon*. Washington, D.C.: Smithsonian Books, 2003.

Henderson, Kim. *50 Simple Steps to Save Our World's Rainforests: How to Save our Rainforests Through Everyday Acts*. Topanga, Calif.: Freedom Press, 2003.

Hildebrandt, Ziporah. *Marina Silva: Defending Rainforest Communities in Brazil*. New York: The Feminist Press at CUNY, 2001.

Knight, Tim. *Journey Into the Rainforest*. New York: Oxford University Press, 2001.

Patent, Dorothy Hinshaw. *Children Save the Rainforest*. New York: Dutton Juvenile, 1996.

Streissguth, Thomas. *Brazil in Pictures*. Minneapolis, Minn.: Lerner Publications, 2003.

## WEB SITES

### National Geographic

*www.nationalgeographic.com*

Provides a wealth of articles and photographs about the rain forest, as well as other natural resources and environmental challenges.

### The Nature Conservancy

*www.natureconservancy.org*

The Web site of this conservation society includes an entire section on tropical rain forests.

**The Rainforest Alliance's Learning Site**

*www.rainforest-alliance.org/education*

The Rainforest Alliance's education page offers many educational resources for learning more about the rain forest.

# Picture Credits

# Index

## A

Agricultural Workers Confederation (CONTAG) 45
Agro-extractive Cooperative 57
Air America 12–14
Alberto, Zé 58
Allegretti, Mary 61, 62
Alliance of Forest Peoples 43, 63
Alves da Silva, Alvarino 93
Alves da Silva, Darli 74, 80–84, 87, 91–93
Alves Pereira, Darci 90, 91–93
Amazon rain forest region
    biodiversity in 14
    Brazil's plan for economic development of 28–30
    as carbon sink 38
    dangers of 25
    overview of 11
    resources of 19
animals, magical 34–35
anthem 77–80
ARENA. *See* National Renovating Alliance

## B

Barros, Raimundo (cousin) 90
Bastos de Moura, Vitalmiro 100
beef industry 38. *See also* Cattle ranching
Better World Society 69
Bezzera, Ilzamar (wife) 59, 71, 84–85, 87
biodiversity, in Amazon rain forest 14
bioprospecting 106
birth of Chico Mendes 20
Boco do Acre 49
Brazil, overview of 10–11

Brazil nuts 23–24, 36, 76
Brazilian Democratic Movement (MDB) 46–47
Brazilian Institute for the Environment and Renewable Natural Resources (IBAMA) 94–96
Brazilian Literacy Movement (MOBRAL) 41–42
Brazilian National Anthem 77–80
bribery 30, 76
British Broadcasting Corporation 12
burning 39, 101. *See also* Slash-and-burn clearing
burning season 36

## C

Cachoeira estate, empate at 74–81
cancer therapies, Amazon rain forest and 19
Cappato, Jorge 30
carbon dioxide 36–39
carbon sinks 37, 39
Cargill 103
Carneiro de Lima, José 48
Carter, Jimmy 68
Catholic Church 46, 48, 54
Catholic Land Pastoral 101
cattle ranching 29–33, 38, 44, 106
Ceará state 20
CEDI. *See* Ecumenical Documentation and Information Center
César Mesquita, Fernando 95
Chico Mendes Extractive Reserve 96
Chico Mendes Institute 105
children 59

Children's Alliance for the
Protection of the Environment 68
clear-cutting. *See* Slash-and-burn
clearing
climate change, deforestation and
36–39
CNS. *See* National Rubber Tappers'
Council
coffee, Amazon rain forest and 19
Cold War 12
conferences 61–63
conspiracies 90–91
CONTAG. *See* Agricultural
Workers Confederation
cooperatives 56–57
Curipira 35

**D**
death of Chico Mendes 87
death threats 47, 82–84, 98
debt-bondage system 18, 20, 56–57
deforestation. *See also* Slash-and-
burn clearing
climate change and 36–39
Indians and 42
laws regulating 76
statistics on 96
Delta Construction Company 76–81
Democratic Ruralist Union (UDR)
65, 83, 90
diseases 29, 43
dogs 25
drought 33, 36, 39
Duke of Edinborough Conservation
Medal 62
Duque Estrada, Joaquim Osório 77

**E**
economic development 28–30,
101–103
Ecuador estate, empate at 74–81
Ecumenical Documentation and
Information Center (CEDI) 54, 55

Ecumenical Services Network 55
education. *See also* Literacy; Rubber
Tappers' Project
debt-bondage system and 18,
21–22
Euclides Fernandes Távora and
12–16, 27
lack of formal 7–8
empates
in Boco do Acre 49
at Ecuador and Cachoeira
74–81
overview of 44–45
retaliation for 72–73
in Xapuri 52
Environmental Defense Fund 61,
63, 66
erosion 33, 76
extractive reserves 64–68, 73, 81,
95–96

**F**
fallow fields 33
Farina, Salvador 65
Feitosa, Maria Eunice (wife) 59
Fernando de Noronho 9
fires, statistics on 72
food, as resource of Amazon rain
forest 19
forestry offices, occupation of 80
forests. *See* Deforestation; Slash-
and-burn clearing
fruits, Amazon rain forest and 19
funeral for Chico Mendes 89

**G**
Gadelha, Jose Moacir 59
Galvao, Regivaldo 100
Giocondo, Dom 46
Global 500 prizes 62, 68, 69
global warming 36–39
Goodall, Jane 68
Gore, Al 39

Goulart, Joao 12
grains, Amazon rain forest and 19
greenhouse gases 36–39
Greenpeace United Kingdom 103
Gross, Tony 98
Guarani, St. John of 35

**H**
health care 58–59
highways 29, 66, 67–68, 72

**I**
IBAMA. *See* Brazilian Institute for
    the Environment and Renewable
    Natural Resources
IDB. *See* Inter-American
    Development Bank
illiteracy 41–42, 54–56
*An Inconvenient Truth* (Gore) 39
indigenous peoples 32, 42–43
Inter-American Development Bank
    (IDB) 66–68

**J**
jaguars 25–26

**L**
labor unions
    Democratic Ruralist Union
        (UDR) 65, 83, 90
    rubber tappers and 15, 44–45
    rural workers' 45–46
    system of in Brazil 46
    Union of Indigenous Nations
        43, 63
    Xapuri Rural Workers' Union
        48–52, 58, 76, 84, 98
Lamb, Robert 69
land ownership 30–31, 44, 65
latex 23. *See also* Rubber tapping
laws 76

literacy 41–42, 54–56
Literate Brazil program 56
loans 66, 67–68
logging, commercial 102, 106
Lopes Filho, Iraci (mother) 20, 27
Lula da Silva, Luiz Inácio 56

**M**
magical animals 34
Malaya 18
Manual da Silva, Francisco 77
marriage 59
MDB. *See* Brazilian Democratic
    Movement
medicinal plants 19, 106
memorial services 89–90
Mendes, Angela (daughter) 59
Mendes, Elenira (daughter) 59,
    104–105
Mendes, Francisco (father) 18, 20,
    23
Mendes, Roseangela (daughter) 59
Mendes, Sandino (son) 59, 104
Mendes, Zuza (brother) 83, 85–86
Mendes Extractive Reserve 96
Mendes Institute 105
MOBRAL. *See* Brazilian Literacy
    Movement
Mother of the Rubber Tree 35
murders
    conspiracy theory for 90–91
    continuing 98, 101
    of Dorothy Stang 99–100, 106
    of Mendes 87, 90–91
    trying to prevent 82
    by UDR as retaliation 65
    of Wilson Pinheiro 49

**N**
national anthem 77–80
National Geographic Society 68
National Plan for Agrarian Reform
    65

National Renovating Alliance (ARENA) 46–47
National Rubber Tappers' Congress 61–63
National Rubber Tappers' Council (CNS) 63, 66, 76, 98
National Wildlife Federation 66
Our Nature initiative 95
newspapers, learning to read from 12
nuts 19, 23–24, 36. *See also* Brazil nuts

**O**

*O Rio Branco* 90–91
Our Nature initiative 95
Oxfam International 55, 57, 61

**P**

Pará state 20, 99–100, 106
Pastoral Land Commission 54
Peter I (Emperor of Brazil) 10
pharmaceutical companies 106
Pinheiro, Wilson 49–51
plants, medicinal 19, 106
policy changes after assassination 94–95
political parties, overview of 46–47
Portugal 10
Prestes, Luis Carlos 9
profitability 106
Projecto Seringuero (Rubber Tappers' Project) 53–57

**Q**

Queen of the Forest 35

**R**

Radio Moscow 12
radio programs 12–14

rainfall 33, 36
Redford, Robert 68
reserves, extractive 64–68, 73, 81, 95–96
Revkin, Andrew 83
*O Rio Branco* 90–91
Rio Branco, mayor of 90
Rio de Janeiro 72
roads 29, 66, 67–68, 72
Rodrigues, Gomercindo 25, 28, 45, 86
Rubber Tappers' Project 53–57
rubber tapping. *See also* Latex
   cattle ranching and 30–32
   daily life and 20–23
   history of 17–18
Rural Workers' Union. *See* Xapuri Rural Workers' Union

**S**

St. John of Guarani 35
saints 35
Sarney, José 94–95
schooling. *See* Education
Schwartzman, Stephen 63, 64, 101, 108
seringals, defined 18
seringueiros, defined 7
Sisters of Notre Dame de Namure 99–100
slash-and-burn clearing 32–33, 36–39, 42
slavery 11
sloths 34
soldados da boirracha 18
soybean farming 102–103
spices, Amazon rain forest and 19
standoffs. *See* Empates
Stang, Dorothy 99–100, 106
subsistence farming 42
Superintendency for the Development of the Amazon (SUDAM) 29–30

sustainability, rubber tapping and
23
sustainable development 62, 64

**T**
Távora, Euclides Fernandes 9,
12–16, 27
Teles de Carvalho, Derci 52
torture 51
trade unions. *See* Unions
Turner, Ted 69

**U**
UDR. *See* Democratic Ruralist
Union
Union of Indigenous Nations
43, 63
unions
Democratic Ruralist Union
(UDR) 65, 83, 90
rubber tappers and 15, 44–45
rural workers' 45–46
system of in Brazil 46
Union of Indigenous Nations
43, 63

Xapuri Rural Workers' Union
48–52, 58, 76, 84, 98
United Nations Environmental
Programme (UNEP) 62, 68, 69

**V**
vanilla beans 19
Vargas, Getúlio 46
vegetables 19
vincristine 19

**W**
Washington, D.C. 67
wildlife 14, 25–26, 34–35
World Bank 101
World War II 18
World Wildlife Federation 62

**X**
Xapuri Rural Workers' Union
48–52, 58, 76, 84, 98

**Z**
zero deforestation plan 103

# About the Author

ALEXA GORDON MURPHY has an M.A. in Professional Writing from the University of Massachusetts at Dartmouth. She has been writing educational books and materials for young people for 10 years. Conserving the rain forest and halting climate change are subjects very near to Murphy's heart. She is a freelance writer and editor, who lives in southern Vermont.